Swallows & Robins
The Guests In My Garden

Susie Kelly

Swallows & Robins
The Guests In My Garden

Susie Kelly

Blackbird Digital Books
London
2012

Blackbird Digital Books

London 2012

First published by Blackbird Digital Books 2012

© Susie Kelly 2012

The moral right of the author has been asserted.

Cover artwork & illustrations by Elle Ford

ISBN-13: 978-1481076449

ISBN-10: 1481076442

To everybody who hates housework

CONTENTS

Chapter 1 1
Chapter 2 10
Chapter 3 18
Chapter 4 26
Chapter 5 35
Chapter 6 41
Chapter 7 47
Chapter 8 56
Chapter 9 62
Chapter 10 72
Chapter 11 75
Chapter 12 81
Chapter 13 85
Chapter 14 96
Chapter 15 121
Chapter 16 126
Chapter 17 142
Chapter 18 143
Chapter 19 148
Chapter 20 .152
Chapter 21 156

Chapter 22 164

Chapter 23 176

Chapter 24 181

Chapter 25 192

Chapter 26 196

Chapter 27 203

Chapter 28 208

Chapter 29 215

Chapter 30 226

Chapter 31 235

Chapter 32 239

Chapter 33 244

Chapter 34 249

Acknowledgements 256

Introduction

OUR Uncle Charlie was a dapper little man who lived with his cat, Tibbles, in a decaying but very large house in a less desirable area of London. Bought for £350 ($570) during the 1960s, despite its current condition and location the property had increased manifold in value and was worth a handsome sum of which we had been allocated a generous portion "when the time came".

Uncle Charlie had not always been little, but he had always been dapper. He was proud of his wartime service as a rear gunner on Lancaster bombers. Several photographs showed a sturdy, fresh-faced fellow in his RAF uniform and later in his demob suit. They bore no discernible similarity to the shrunken body and shiny head sitting in the armchair he had bought in 1956. Tibbles was the beneficiary of all the devotion and admiration that Uncle Charlie had once given to his wife, who had died twenty years previously and whom everybody who knew her agreed had been a spiteful cow. He was passionately supportive of Tottenham Hotspur football club, and anxious that when he passed through his own heavenly goalposts his wealth should be well and wisely spent.

Each time we visited Uncle Charlie his clothes looked another size too large, but his shirt was still crisp and white, his tie perfectly knotted, and his blazer buttons polished.

"Promise me," he said, reaching out with a clawed little hand, "promise you won't go frittering it away when I'm gone. Use it for something sensible."

We promised.

Eventually Uncle Charlie became so small that he simply vanished, leaving behind a small rectangular hump of earth, two tiny bunches of flowers, and the pot of money which we were honour bound to spend sensibly.

Up there on his celestial cloud, would Uncle Charlie regard a six-month world cruise as a sensible investment? It would broaden our horizons, allow us to visit new places, meet new people, learn new cultures, eat good food and not have to do anything demanding or energetic. It was almost certain that we would never again have such an opportunity.

On the other hand two ancient buildings on our property, originally houses, latterly used as a garage and stable, currently occupied by various wildlife, were falling down. Decades of frost, wind and rainfall had toppled the chimneys. The roofs had caved in, the walls were cracking apart, and the rain was flushing away the mud and animal muck that precariously held the remaining stones in place. Soon they would be reduced to piles of rubble to be removed at vast expense.

So the cruise was off. Instead of travelling around the world meeting new people, they would be coming to us, bringing with them their hopes, habits, hang-ups and idiosyncrasies. Many became friends for life. Some came and went almost unnoticed. Others left lasting impressions. Terry, my husband, has always said that I am like a magnet for crackpots, and certainly a number of them managed to make their way here. Meet the swallows and robins – our summer and winter visitors. At the time there were some whom I could have happily battered to bits with a shovel, but now, after many years have passed I can look back on them all, perhaps ruefully, but certainly with affection.

Chapter One
Year One – First Find Your Builder

THE work required to convert the buildings is enormous, and our inheritance will have to be managed with atomic precision. Artisan builders are beyond our means. We must put our trust and money into a one-man, jack-of-all-trades outfit. The saying about peanuts and monkeys rings in my ears.

Living here on my own for much of the time, while Terry works in England, the responsibility for organising and feeding the monkey rests on me, and I admit that I am daunted. I've heard terrible stories about builders. I don't like fights, shouting, threats, aggravation of any kind and will go to considerable lengths to avoid it. I will willingly drive back and forth to builders' merchants for sacks of cement, timber and any other materials; within the limits of my physical strength I will hold, lug and lift things. I will supply tea and/or coffee willingly, and in copious amounts, and I will pay, promptly, the agreed number of peanuts. In return I will not expect miracles, but an honest day's work, each and every day, resulting in two habitable buildings.

Some friends have recommended a retired French stonemason who can also turn his hand to roofing. He arrives by moped, with a ragged cigarette clenched between his lips. He is very tiny like a marmoset, with round, rheumy eyes and tufts of hair burgeoning from his ears and nose. He is surprisingly strong for his size, and agile for his age. He heaves stones and timbers, and shovels rubble into wheelbarrows; his friend comes and takes away the rubble in a trailer. At exactly 12 noon each day, the marmoset lays down his tools and takes out from his overall an Opinel knife, and from a box on his moped an evil-smelling garlic sausage, a baguette and a bottle of red wine. He sits down on a bench in the garden, munches methodically, drinks the bottle of wine, accepts a small cup of black coffee, comments on the weather, disappears to the end of the field behind a hedge, and at precisely 1.30 pm is back at work. By the end of the first week reusable stones and timbers are neatly stacked, and most of the rubble has gone. Maurice the marmoset is polite, respectful, knows what he's doing and gets on and does it. What more could we want?

He doesn't arrive on Monday morning of the second week, and his telephone is unanswered. Late in the afternoon his friend comes to say that Maurice has fallen off his moped and broken two fingers. He will not be able to continue working. This is a real blow. The friend cannot recommend anybody else to take his place.

I search for a new monkey. One wants too many peanuts, and one cannot start for at least two months. That only leaves a stubbly-jawed, stocky fellow with muscles and an insolent attitude. He starts his working day with a picnic in the back of his old van, drinking half of a bottle of red wine and eating a tin of sardines. At noon, he finishes the bottle and chops chunks of cheese onto a baguette. By early afternoon his breath can kill at fifty paces. Like Maurice he's a good worker, but he has several times referred to my "belles fesses," and when I look it up in the dictionary I find it means nice bum. It is only a matter of time – three days to be precise – before he lunges at me, pins me to a wall and nearly suffocates me with his toxic breath. I shout to the dogs – we have five and he is nervous of them – and when I have re-established my composure I pay him off.

Next is an English jack-of-all trades who promises much. After two days, even as a novice myself I can see that he is out of his depth and doesn't know where to start or what to do. He sits in the garden and makes lists and orders materials and sketches plans and drinks litres of coffee, but after two weeks nothing much has changed. There are piles of materials all over the place and two windows put into the upstairs of the larger cottage. Something about them doesn't look right, but I can't put my finger on exactly what. He had promised the properties would both be ready by mid-July – that's in four months' time. Now he is talking of "trying to get one ready this year, and finishing the other next year."

I am a failure as a project manager/monkey handler. Paying Jack-of-all-trades his weekly peanut ration hurts, because he is not earning it. My neighbour tells me that if I go out, Jack sits in the garden sunbathing. When I find him loading some of our timber into the back of his van before he leaves one evening, I am not convinced by his explanation that he is putting it there to keep it dry. We have words. He unloads it with bad grace, and chucks it in a puddle. We part on terms of mutual dislike.

With bookings already filling up most of the summer, I've started spending the deposit money to boost the building fund which is running low. I'm frantic.

An acquaintance introduces a big, broad-shouldered man with a disconcerting mannerism of looking over his own right shoulder when he talks, so that I speak to the side of his head. Wandering around the buildings, he pushes at the walls with his hands as if he expects them to

3

fall down, scrapes with his foot at the floors, tutting and shaking his head.

"When were you wanting these places ready?"

"Our first bookings are for the second week of July."

He opens his eyes wide, then makes a puffing noise through pouted lips.

"Well, we'd better get on with it. What you need here is hands, and plenty of them."

I feel a glimmer of hope.

Next day he starts work, bringing with him his girlfriend, her brother and cousin, and two small dogs. One of them is adept at climbing ladders and scrambling about on beams, while the other, which is not, sits howling and whimpering in frustration.

No 4, as I mentally call him, is terrifyingly gung-ho. He prowls around with a screeching chainsaw searching for something to chop or lop. This morning he's up an oak sawing through the 12" trunk of ivy that is throttling the tree. He is balanced precariously on a branch, thrashing around with the machine like something from a horror film. Then he attacks some discarded beams, and chops them into slices for firewood. When he has run out of anything more to chop, he starts rectifying the mess created and left behind by monkey No. 3.

Addressing the two windows that have been perplexing me, he points out that they have no lintels, and are supporting the entire roof. They will have to come out, he says, and be replaced properly. But if he takes them out, won't the roof collapse, I ask. He taps the side of his nose, and tells me not to worry.

4

This chap is no monkey. He knows what he's doing, and he's getting on with it. He's quickly made himself at home, bounding into the kitchen every morning promptly at 8.00 am, whistling tunelessly and making himself and me a cup of Earl Grey and two slices of buttered toast, plus various refreshments for his team. They are hearty eaters and as they are all working for No. 4 and not being paid by me, I'm happy to keep them well fed.

With eleven weeks of bookings for the season, and work progressing as it is, we are well on schedule.

The peanut supply is diminishing rapidly, and we still have to furnish the cottages. I've bought new beds, cookers and fridges, and some easy chairs, but we need much more. I find a card in a local supermarket advertising "Quality furniture at sensible prices," and call the number.

A deep public school voice instructs: "If you wish to speak to Beverly, then please say so. If you wish to speak to Tristram, do so now."

I explain that I'm looking for decent inexpensive furniture for our holiday guests, and Tristram assures me that he has a warehouse of furniture that will be exactly what I am looking for. We arrange to meet twelve miles away at a place I have never heard of. He will wait for me at the crossroads, because, he assures me cheerfully, I'll never find his house by myself.

After driving through an endless network of narrow roads, past collections of houses where no sign of life stirs, numerous fields and scraggy copses, I am relieved to see an estate car parked at the agreed rendezvous with a man leaning against it. But not a man like any other. In bloodstock terms, he is 'by Viking out of Greek Goddess'.

He's tall and slender. His skin is the same golden copper as his cropped hair and trimmed beard. His blue eyes are fringed with thick black lashes. His nose is straight and narrow, and his broad smile shows startling white teeth. As I climb out of the car my leg bones threaten to melt. I offer a hot, sticky little paw to the outstretched golden hand with its slender fingers, and stand there foolishly and speechlessly.

"Do you like dogs?" he asks, opening the door of his car and releasing a torrent of smooth-haired dachshunds, sleek as otters.

"Meet the children. Children, say hello to our new friend."

The dogs prod my ankles with wet noses, tails wagging.

"Good. The children approve. Let's go."

He invites the children back into his car, and I follow him along a bumpy path through thick woods sinister in their dark stillness, quelling a momentary feeling of panic. What if he's a murderer or rapist? Nobody knows I'm here. They'll never find my body. Who will feed my animals? Even if I manage to escape, I'll never find my way back.

We break out of the woods into a field, and the path leads to a gravelled area in front of a house typical of the area, long and low, with two front doors and a pantiled roof. The walls are a light shade of apricot, the shutters a soft eau-de-nil.

Uncannily, as he opens my car door, Tristram says: "I expect you were getting worried about where you were going to end up!"

He ushers me into the living room. "Come."

After living on a building site for so long, I've almost forgotten what a normal home looks like. There are a few oriental rugs scattered on the flags, a couple of sofas flanking the fireplace, a pile of books on a low table. It's simple, comfortable, and tasteful.

"Be at home," says Tristram, waving a beautiful hand around vaguely.

"I expect you would love a glass of mint tea. Beverly! Come and meet our guest."

Through the patio doors comes a slightly older man - as blonde as Tristram, but shorter, stockier, clean-shaven, with smiling eyes.

"My partner," says Tristram. "Beverly, show Susie your garden. I shall join you shortly with something heavenly."

Beverly leads me through sliding glass doors onto a patio surrounded by flowerbeds, pergolas, climbing roses, a small pond, herbaceous borders and a bright green, velvety lawn. The smell of roses and honeysuckle fills the air. It's a perfect English country garden, in the middle of rural France - something that takes great skill and patience to achieve. Colours and shapes blend in harmony. We sit under a gazebo on a paved area.

"Are you a professional garden designer?" I ask. "It's heavenly."

"I was an accountant by profession, but a gardener at heart. It's taken me four years to create this. I've had to adapt many of my ideas – the climate here is too extreme for certain plants, but yes, I'm rather proud and pleased with the result."

It's an idyllic location, secluded and with unhindered views of fields and open countryside.

"It suits us, my dear. It's private."

Tristram arrives with frosted glasses of chilled mint tea, and we sit chatting while the children wrestle playfully around our feet.

"No, Pumpkin," he calls to one of the dogs who is tentatively trying to excavate a clump of campanula from between some edging stones.

"Shall we visit the emporium?" he asks when we've finished our tea.

"What is it you're after exactly?"

"Basic, practical stuff. Dining tables and chairs, side tables, book cases. It must be decent, but not expensive. Our budget's very tight."

"Right. Let's see what we've got." He leads the way to a large barn at right angles to the house, and hauls back a sliding door.

Daylight floods in onto stacks of packing crates and bulky shapes draped in blankets.

"That's the good stuff that keeps the wolf from the door. Over here is the rest."

There are acres of items of furniture, arranged in neat rows. It's a mixed bag: formica kitchen units with chrome dials, battered pine tables, chairs that need re-caning, baths, stoves, garden furniture, but also some relatively modern items.

"House clearances. Usually there will be at least a couple of good pieces that I sell on to dealers. And the rest, this kind of thing, well, you'd be surprised, but it goes, sooner or later. I've a contact who buys for film and TV sets. They're always looking out for stuff like this. And 60s items are coming into fashion again out here."

I pick out some basic items that, with a bit of love and effort, will do for the time being. Tristram will deliver them when I'm ready, for "a small consideration. " I don't like to ask how small.

As I drive away, he and Beverly wave from the doorway, standing beside each other, with the children at their feet. A scene of contentment and domestic bliss that gives me a warm fuzzy feeling.

Chapter Two
Year One – The Gravel Mountain

BY the end of April progress has slackened. Although the roofs, windows and doors are in place, the buildings are still empty shells. No. 4 insists there is no cause to worry. He has reduced his workforce to just himself and his girlfriend, who survives on a strict diet of coffee and Gitanes. She is as thin as a reed but impressively nimble and strong, carrying and lifting hods of tiles and buckets of cement without damaging her immaculate manicure or creasing her face. Sometimes it almost seems as if she is working harder than he is.

By the end of May the electrics and water services are all in place, but I am waking in a panic almost every night. A month doesn't seem long enough to tile the floors, put up the pine ceilings and paint the whole place, not to mention clearing up the mess outside and getting the garden planted. No. 4's girlfriend has disappeared, taking the small sad dog with her. Pouring his 20th cup of tea of the day, licking and dabbing his fingers into the biscuit box to mop up the last remaining crumbs, No. 4 promises we have time to spare. I should learn to relax and have faith. I want to, but I can't. He is constantly up and down and backwards and forwards. The chainsaw is always buzzing and the biscuit tin always empty and the tea always brewing, but I can't see any noticeable progress in the cottages.

Less than three weeks before the first guests arrive, No 4 leaves a phone message to say he and his girlfriend have taken the dogs on holiday "to the seaside," as the howling dog is suffering from depression. Both the cottages look like bombsites, with ladders, tools and sacks of plaster all over the place. I am now seriously stressed and can feel the blood pulsing in my ears and pumping around my body faster than it should. I trundle around with a wheelbarrow collecting rocks, broken tiles, lumps of superfluous concrete, bits of timber and lengths of cable and pipe, shovelling them into sacks to take to the tip. No 4's mobile phone is switched off, and his girlfriend's parents have no idea when they are likely to return. I consider taking up smoking.

Three days later, unrepentant and infuriatingly patronising, No. 4 returns with his ladder-climbing dog. He ignores my displeasure and actually pats me on the head, suggesting I bake a cake while he gets on with his work. In a fit of extreme pique I hide all biscuits and Earl Grey tea bags. Shortly afterwards he bounces chirpily into the kitchen, singing his monotonous five-note tune, and clicking the kettle on. Then there is much opening and closing of drawers, and finally he comes into the living room to say he can't find the tea bags. I tell him that until there is some visible progress on the building front, tea and biscuits are off the menu. He shrugs and bounces out again, humming. I don't see him for the rest of the day. I lay awake most of the night terrified he won't turn up in the morning.

Promptly at 8.00 am he arrives, singing 'zippetty doo da,' waving a box of tea bags and a bag of pains au chocolat. Today, he announces, he will be tiling the floors while I make the tea. At the end of the day he can barely walk, but to his credit the entire ground floor of both buildings has been perfectly tiled. And he has had a

11

brainwave, an inspiration, for a time-saving, labour-saving way of grouting them. Instead of the conventional laborious mixing of grout and spreading into the joints with a scraper, he will pour a very wet cement mix over the entire floor, allowing it to flow into the cracks. Once it has set and dried, he will wipe over the tiles with a cloth to remove the excess. He estimates this could save two days work. I'm apprehensive at the thought of the floors smothered in wet cement, but we desperately need to save time.

Next morning he is sloshing buckets of runny cement all over the newly tiled floors. The liquid doesn't flow, but lays in a sullen grey puddle. We have to wade about in it and push it around with lengths of wood, and it makes a simply dreadful mess. By next day it has formed a thick gritty coating covering the entire ground floor of both buildings. After rubbing vigorously with a dry cloth, No 4 admits gloomily that it hasn't worked out quite as he hoped. He won't have time to rectify it as well as fitting the kitchens and ceiling panelling and painting all the walls. He passes the floor problem to me.

It takes three days, with buckets of soapy water, cloths, scrubbing brushes and abrasive pads. While the tiles are wet it looks as if all traces of cement have gone, but as soon as they dry a new grey veil emerges. I have to continually wet the cement and rub it very hard to make any impression, whilst avoiding rubbing the cracks because the grouting is still soft and smears itself over the tiles into a new mess. And hour after hour the humming continues as No 4 makes endless tea, as I am permanently bent double and there are still acres of floor to clean. Scrubbing and rubbing, I start hating No 4 with a fearsome passion.

By the end of the week the kitchen units are installed, the ceilings are in place, and the floors are as clean and free of cement as they are ever going to be. No 4 has done well, and when he comes for his weekly wages he asks whether he may have an advance against his next and final week, as he has a problem with his car and is short of cash. I make an exception to my primal rule of never paying a builder before the work is completed. In spite of everything, he has accomplished almost all that I have asked, so I pay him for the following week.

Next week he will be back to paint all the walls, and fill the courtyards with the twelve cubic yards of crushed limestone he has ordered for the purpose.

When he hasn't shown by mid-day on Monday, and his mobile phone is switched off, I know I've been taken for a ride and have only myself to blame. I begin painting, and I paint from early morning to the small hours of the following morning, until I can barely see, but I get the first coat on the ceilings and walls in both cottages. After a few hours sleep I pick flakes of paint out of my hair and off my face and hands, and start all over again.

The gravel didn't arrive this morning as promised. I call the quarry, who say the delivery is on its way.

Late in the afternoon a truck arrives and begins spewing a mountain of large sharp grey granite pieces. Shouting, waving my arms and making violent throat-slashing signs, I manage to stop the cascade. Half of it is already spreading over the drive. The surly driver insists I ordered granite, not limestone. I call the quarry and they ask me to pass him the phone. After some furious conversation he shovels the stuff back onto his truck and drives away spitting curses and muttering "quelle pute anglaise." The quarry phone back to say they will be here at 9.00 am tomorrow with the limestone.

The following morning they phone again, saying the truck has broken down, and then in the afternoon they are short of a driver, but they'll be here tomorrow morning without fail.

I'm woken next day by a crashing and whooshing noise. It sounds as if the buildings are collapsing. Leaping to the window I see a vast truck expelling a torrent of crushed limestone just inside the gate. And as I watch another truck drives up and spews out a second heap, forming a mountain range which cuts off my car, house and the cottages from the rest of the world. There is enough gravel to give the entire hamlet a generous coating.

It's already hot. The air is still. The only sounds are the droning of the bees and chirping of the crickets. I find No. 4's shovel, and a battered wheelbarrow, and start shovelling and tipping. The gravel is only about twenty yards from where it needs to go, but it might as well be twenty miles. The shovel is heavy and the limestone is heavy and the wheelbarrow is heavy. After two hours, it is impossibly hot. The tarmac is melting. The garden is wilting. I can barely lift the shovel. Every few minutes I step back from the pile to see if there is any noticeable difference. There isn't. I recognise the impossibility of moving it all by tomorrow. Staring at it bleakly, I curse No 4 with an intensity that frightens me. Then I burst into tears of rage and frustration.

What am I going to do? I bawl. The dogs sniff and lick me as I sit on the pile, jabbing my heels angrily into the stones.

A car engine stops on the other side of the gravel mountain. There's a lot of crunching, and over the top appears Tristram who slithers down onto the driveway. I'd forgotten he's delivering the furniture today.

"My dear girl, what on earth has happened? What have you done? You look dreadful!"

I throw myself at him, sobbing, and waving hopelessly at the heap of limestone.

"Why don't we have a lovely glass of mint tea?" he asks, tactfully disentangling my damp dirty hands from his crisp white shirt. "You'll find it really does make everything better."

By the time I have picked some mint, torn it up, put it in the pot, sprinkled it with sugar and left it to steep, Tristram has taken off his shirt and is shovelling heroically, singing snatches from Rigoletto in his deep baritone. I want to fling my arms around him again and kiss him all over, but I'm not sure he'd appreciate it.

"I've given Bev a call. He'll be here soon."

Beverly arrives with the children, who make instant friends with our very sociable dogs and go and lie in the cool of the house with them. We dig out a second wheelbarrow and another shovel, and between the two of them, fuelled with gallons of mint tea and cucumber and tomato sandwiches, by late afternoon the mountain has been moved and the courtyards are carpeted with nearly knee-deep limestone chippings. There is no time to hire a compactor, and anyway it wouldn't be any use. As Tristram points out after we have bashed at the stuff with the back of the shovels and jumped up and down on it to no effect, there is far too much of it.

"Why did you order so much? And it's the wrong grade, far too coarse. It will never compact into a smooth surface."

"It's going to be hell to walk on," Beverly adds helpfully.

As a matter of fact, it's virtually impossible. Like trudging over very deep, very thick sand. As you drag your feet out your shoes fill with little pebbles. We stare gloomily at it, willing it to vanish. Tristram remarks playfully that it will certainly anchor the garden furniture in place.

They are both streaked with dust and sweat.

"You won't mind if we rinse ourselves off?" Tristram points to our garden hosepipe.

"Perhaps you'd like me to do your backs?" I suggest.

"Get thee behind us, Satan!" he laughs. "And make more mint tea."

Once they're refreshed, we unload the furniture and put it in place. It looks better than I had expected.

"Nice. Most pleasant. Your guests will love it here," says Beverly. "It's a lovely location. I can give you some plants, too, so that you can pretty the garden. I've plenty of cuttings and seedlings."

Later we sit by candlelight listening to the nightingales, eating a Greek salad and sipping, as a change from mint tea, a bottle of Sancerre that Beverly thoughtfully brought with him. I reflect on how very lucky and privileged I am to count as friends these two kind and charming men.

"Do the cottages have names?" asks Beverly.

"Yes. The larger one is Lavande, and the little one Pissenlit. I've got a couple of ceramic name plaques on order."

They both look rather startled. "Pissenlit? Do you know what that means?"

"Yes. It's French for dandelion," I say, straight-faced.

"But surely you know how it actually translates," insists Beverly.

"No," I lie. "Tell me."

Beverly coughs. "Well, literally, it means 'piss in the bed'."

"Well I never. I hope nobody does," I reply.

Tristram catches my eye. "Naughty! You knew perfectly well. I think you have a somewhat contorted sense of humour."

Neither he nor Beverly will accept anything for their help today.

"An absolute pleasure. And any time you are in need, you have only to ask."

It's 11.00pm by the time they leave. The last thing I have to do is varnish the staircases in both cottages. It only takes an hour. The brush starts falling to pieces, and a few bristles remain embedded for eternity in the varnish, like insects in amber. But I don't think anybody will notice. We're open for business!

Chapter Three

Year One – First Guests

APART from one of the cats having diarrhoea behind the washing machine, everything is under control and organised. I've put a dozen pots of vivid geraniums in each courtyard, set up the garden furniture and barbecues, and filled vases with sunflowers, welcome baskets with tea, coffee and fruit, and the fridge with croissants, butter, jam, milk and a bottle of wine. There are stacks of brochures on local attractions, lists of recommended restaurants, a pile of books and board games. By early afternoon, we are ready for our first guests, six young men who have booked Lavande for a fortnight. Does this portend drunken orgies, blaring rap music and a smashed-up house? Is it going to be a baptism of fire for a novice landlady?

Confusingly they all look virtually identical when they arrive, like a litter of puppies. All with neat hair cuts, all wearing odd, low-slung, baggy shorts, trainers and T-shirts with slogans on them: Out of my mind - back shortly. Rich bitch wanted - apply here. Save water - drink beer.

They politely shake hands and introduce themselves. Three of them are called Chris: Tall Chris, Skinny Chris and Chris, who is also tall. They all thank me for having them, and unload half a dozen cardboard cartons from the back of their people carrier.

An hour later barbecue scents waft into the air, and I can hear bottles chinking. Apart from conversation and laughter, and sometimes the clink of glass or popping of a cork, that's all the noise I hear from the cottage during their stay. Occasionally they pile into their car and disappear for a couple of hours, and they spend a whole day at Monkey Valley, but mostly they just hang around in the garden, playing with the cats, chatting and laughing. Twice they offer to take the dogs for a walk, and once they ask if I need anything from town. Every day they neatly peg out their washing on the line. I'd love to know what they do in real life, but if guests don't volunteer information, I don't ask.

When they leave at the end of the fortnight, they knock on the door to say farewell, thank me for having them, tell me they all love the cats, and present me with an enormous fruit tart and a little card that says: "Thank you, missus. We've had a great time. See you next year."

In the guest book each of them has written, in different coloured ink, some vertically, and one diagonally across the page: "I love monkeys. And cats." They've left Lavande looking like a show home. They've even cleaned the windows, and left behind in the fridge an unopened bottle of wine, some butter, a packet of bacon, a few bits of fruit and some salad. In the living room I find neat piles of paperback books and magazines with a note saying they hope future guests will enjoy them.

I notice that the varnish on the staircase is peeling off in a few places and looks rather scabby. So I have a good idea – I will rub it down with sandpaper and quickly put a new coat on. The tin says it dries in an hour. But it doesn't. It's still tacky at 4.00pm. Maybe I didn't stir the tin thoroughly enough? By six it's touch dry, but when I prod it with a matchstick, it leaves a small dip. Perhaps it wasn't meant for staircases.

It's almost 8.00pm when an elderly Mercedes pulls up and out climbs a big, shambling man with lank grey hair, and a dainty woman with a blonde elfin hairstyle, peaches and cream complexion and chic, with expensive rings on every finger, a necklace, several bracelets, a brooch and dangling earrings, and a voice that could shatter glass at half a mile.

The chic lady introduces them: Alice and Dick. "Let's get to know you," she suggests. "We'll have a drink with you while we recover from the journey."

Scrunching over the courtyard towards the patio, Alice says forthrightly, "Oh, I don't like this gravel. It's going to ruin my shoes." She bends her shapely leg to examine the heels of her stilettos, and her short tight skirt rises to reveal some black and red lacy suspenders. She is either unaware, or unabashed.

"Would you like tea?" I ask.

"I'll have a beer," replies Dick. "In fact," he laughs, "I'll have a couple."

"You'll go and get my Burberry bag out of the car first," Alice tells him. He heaves himself up onto his slightly bowed legs entwined with thick, triffid-like veins. Long yellow toenails poking out from his sandals remind me of Rosa Kreb's shoes with the daggers in the toes in 'From Russia with Love'.

Alice must have caught my expression, because as he ambles towards the gate she says, "Not beautiful, is he? But very useful when I need a chauffeur and porter. And very obedient. Never underestimate the value of an ugly man. " She wiggles her little finger, and winks.

"What would you like to drink?" I ask, and intending to continue "tea, coffee, soft drink or beer?" But Alice beats me to it.

"I'll have a Nuits-St-Georges if you have some. In a big glass, please. I always have a big glass."

I gulp and apologise that we do not have any Nuits-St-Georges. The best I can offer her is an excellent Sauvignon from the Domaine de Villemont, an Haut Poitou vineyard about 30 miles away. It is in the fridge waiting for a special occasion. But I somehow can't bring myself to offer Alice the cheap plonk we keep for every day.

Sprawling in his chair, Dick knocks back his first beer with one slurp and tosses the empty bottle into a flowerbed with a belch. I try not to look at his feet.

Alice sniffs her wine, swirls it around the glass, sips, sucks, and says, "Hm. I wouldn't buy it, personally, but it'll do. Dick will have to get me some St Georges tomorrow." She gulps it down and holds out her glass for a refill. With every move she makes, her jewellery jangles a merry little tune like a tastefully decorated musical Christmas tree. The only time she isn't talking is when she's drinking.

I mention the staircase, and ask if they would mind very much not walking on it in their shoes until tomorrow, when it should be completely dry.

"It will be fine with bare feet, but I think the surface is still just a little soft and might not stand up to shoes."

"My darling daughter," Alice says, "has a very expensive house. She earns a huge salary; so does her husband. Both their children are gifted and go to private schools, don't they Dick? She's had the whole house redecorated by the most exclusive company in the south of England. Hand-made oak kitchen units; real marble floors in the bathrooms - there are four bathrooms, aren't there, Dick?"

She twitters on for several minutes. Dick holds out his empty bottle to me, saying "Top up, love."

While I'm in the kitchen Alice's chattering continues unabated, all about her daughter's splendid house, the landscaped gardens and covered swimming pool.

"Of course, she has a contractor to deal with it. She doesn't have time, and neither does Alan. They have very important jobs. A man comes in to do the cleaning and service the pumps and filters. And of course, he has to make sure that the PHD of the water is just right, doesn't he Dick? I think it's the PHD. Anyway, it's something like that."

Dick grunts and mutters under his breath: "pH, you silly tart."

Alice ignores him.

"Did she have her staircase varnished?" I ask, trying to form a link between our staircase and her daughter.

"Of course not. The cleaner waxes it. It's Jacobean oak."

When there are no beers left in the fridge, and the Sauvignon bottle is empty, I take them over to Lavande.

"Pretty. Nice colour scheme. My darling daughter..."

I nip her daughter quickly in the bud and show them around. We all take off our shoes to go upstairs, and none of us stick to the steps.

Dick has become rather red-faced and loud, and pulls Alice towards him, then bends her over the back of the settee and tries to heave her skirt up.

"Behave yourself, you old goat," she snaps, but she gives me a wink.

"Can't get enough. I've always had that effect on men. Dick knows, don't you Dick?"

"Well, I'll leave you to settle in. Please give me a shout if you need anything – and if you could please remember about taking off your shoes on the staircase."

Alice assures me that they'll take off their shoes, then she flicks a finger at Dick and says, "Go and get the rest of my things in from the car, and make us something to eat. I'm going to do my nails."

I eat a packet of biscuits, take a quick shower then climb into to bed, falling asleep the moment I close my eyes. Later a frightful noise rends the night and wakes me with a start. Tannhauser, at full volume. My watch says 3.25 am. The noise goes on for hours. The dogs howl in harmony. It sounds as if Dick and Alice are settling in nicely.

Next morning, sitting bleary-eyed in the garden sipping coffee and inhaling the early sunshine, with the dogs and cats at my feet, I hear Dick and Alice's car disappearing down the road, and drowse for an hour, enjoying an opportunity to relax.

Our first Pissenlit guests missed their flight from Belfast to London, and consequently don't arrive until mid-afternoon on Sunday. James and Ellen are a young recently-married couple from Belfast, who don't want to be in their home town during the Orange Day parade.

"Things happen, you know. It can get violent. We don't like that sort of thing."

James' broad accent takes a while to get to grips with, but once I tune in I find it seductive. Ellen speaks very softly, in a similar accent, and never takes her eyes from his cheerful face.

"Will you look at that!" He points to a large bumblebee creature exploring a crevice in the wall.

"It's got a red arse! Did you ever hear of a red-arsed bumblebee before?"

He breaks off a lavender stalk and tries to encourage the creature onto it, but after a few moments it buzzes away. James shakes his head in wonderment. "Well, I never. A bloody red-arsed bee."

After they've unpacked, they wander into the garden and ask if they may have a look round. They are both townies, and while Ellen is very timid, James is fearless, loves the dogs and is fascinated by wildlife. Neither have ever had a pet, and James has asked if they can "adopt" the dogs while they're here. The dogs need no enticement. They'll worship anybody who says "Hello," particularly if there's anything edible within range. James holds Ellen by the hand and reassures her while the dogs snuffle around her. She has absolute faith in James. I think if he told her to jump from the roof so that he could catch her, she wouldn't hesitate.

Next he's off to meet the horses, trotting right up behind one of them and patting her on the backside, startling her. Thankfully our two old mares are as gentle as kittens, but I suggest that they might be better approached from the front end.

"Would they be needing a brushing?" asks James. With their glossy summer coats they look spotless and polished, but I give him a body brush and leave him happily brushing and chattering away, with Ellen watching apprehensively from behind the gate.

Alice and Dick return with a car-load of shopping bags. Alice is already chattering before she gets out of the car. From twenty yards I can see her mouth moving non-stop. "...said to him that if he wants me to go to the Gambia with him, I'll need the right clothes. We found a beautiful boutique - very expensive - and he bought me four chiffon blouses. So chic, and terribly useful. You can wear them with anything. And two pairs of flat shoes - one black, one gold. So adaptable. Oh, by the way, I forgot about the stairs and walked on them yesterday evening with my shoes. But I don't think I've done any damage. Dick, go and pour me a big glass of Muscadet."

I love her style.

The Ride of the Valkyries jerks me awake just after 2.00 am. 15 minutes later a broad Irish voice calls out politely across the courtyard. "I wonder could you turn that fecking noise down, please. No offence, friends, but we're trying to sleep."

Alice's fingernail-on-blackboard voice screeches back: "So sorry. We're sozzled. Go to sleep, my love. Dick, turn it off."

Dick mumbles loudly and crashes into something, cursing, and after a few seconds silence reigns. Bliss.

Chapter Four

Year One – Jars of Jam and Pots of Pepper

"MY shoes are ruined. Just look!"

Dressed in minute white shorts - great legs for a woman of her age - a transparent black chiffon top over a black and red lacy bra, and red peep-toe shoes with 4" heels, Alice is waving a pair of delicate golden ballerina shoes.

"Look at the soles! It's all this gravel you've got everywhere. You'll have to get rid of it."

Yes, of course. I'll just run and get a shovel and bucket and take it away - all twelve cubic yards of it.

Dick strolls over. The Old Virginia wafting from his pipe takes me back to my childhood, when my father was seldom without a pipe clenched between his teeth, and his clothing smelt comfortingly of tobacco.

"You're invited to dinner on Thursday," says Alice. "Dick's a wonderful cook, aren't you Dick? Seven thirty for cocktails. Don't be late. Wear something pretty - get rid of those jeans. And put your hair up - it'll take years off you. Dick, get me a drink."

I mention that I'm a vegetarian, but will eat fish. Dick snorts.

"Shut up," snaps Alice. "Well, personally I think vegetarians are a bit cranky, but to each his own. Dick cooks fish beautifully, don't you Dick? Drink, Dick. Now, please."

She rolls her eyes as he shambles away.

I can't help liking Alice. She's genuinely warm-hearted and well-meaning, and she's got Dick trained to a T.

It's past 11.00am next day when James and Ellen emerge from Pissenlit while I'm watering the geraniums.

"Top of the morning! Sorry to be up so late," shouts James.

I assure them that their time is entirely their own, and there is no regulatory getting-up time.

"Do you know," says James, "at home in Belfast we're always awake by 7.00am? We wake naturally. But we slept like wee ones last night, and only woke half an hour ago. It's so quiet. Magic. Oh, now will you look at that!" He points to a lizard basking on the doorstep.

Their pleasure in being here delights me. We need the money, that's for sure, but in my new role as a landlady, rather to my surprise I've realised that the most important thing is knowing that our guests have truly enjoyed their stay.

The weather couldn't be more perfect for holidaymakers, with clear blue skies, temperatures in the low 30s and the faintest breeze. Alice and Derek spend all day every day shopping, and their evenings sitting on the patio eating, drinking, listening to classical music - now played at an acceptable level - and arguing. There is no nook or cranny where Alice's piercing voice cannot be heard.

James and Ellen, meanwhile, sit and read, roam around the garden holding hands, fuss the dogs, buy fresh croissants for the horses every morning, collect eggs from our chickens for their breakfast and feed bacon rinds to the cats. They spend the afternoons behind closed shutters. They've been married less than a year, and are eager to start a family. I wouldn't be surprised if they succeed while they're here.

James marvels that they can pick raspberries right outside their door, and strawberries, lettuce, tomatoes from the vegetable garden. He watches the swallows hunting above the pond, and the bats swooping at dusk. He asks to borrow a book on identifying birds, and buys a small notebook to record all those creatures he has seen or heard - woodpeckers, thrushes, blackbirds, blue tits, hoopoes, nightingales, owls. At night he sits up shining a torch into the undergrowth, spotting hedgehogs and "wee furry things with long tails." He overturns stones and bits of wood to reveal salamanders and toads, and videos the frogs in the pond while they hunt for insects foolhardy enough to go within range. He is open-mouthed with amazement when I tell him that a frog's tongue is attached at the front of its mouth, instead of at the back, so that it can flip it forward with astonishing speed to catch its prey. He spends hours sitting motionless beside the pond with his video camera, until with a joyful yell he jumps up, and shouts: "Oh yessss! I've seen it with my own eyes, and here it is on film. The little green fellow catching a butterfly!"

"It's just a wonderful place you have here," he says. "You're so lucky, so you are. It's another world entirely from the one we live in at home. You can breathe here, and look at the roads – there's nothing on them! You've no stress."

He's right. Compared with the working lives of the average Briton, a few weeks of fighting builders and wrestling tons of pebbles isn't worth complaining about. I'm glad he's opened my eyes again to how fortunate I am. It's too easy to take for granted the space, peace, clean air and easy lifestyle we enjoy.

On Thursday evening I dress in my best, and with my hair piled up, present myself to Alice and Dick at 7.35 pm - never arrive exactly on time: it's frightfully bad manners.

"You're late," says Alice, looking me up and down. "Still, you've made an effort so we'll forgive you. Take a pew."

She waves me to a chair on their patio. It looks enchanting, with wild flowers scattered over the table and scented candles floating in glass bowls.

While Alice and I make inroads into the wine and she fills in the gaps in my knowledge about her wonderful daughter and gifted grandchildren, Dick is preparing food in the kitchen. He sniffs loudly and runs his forearm beneath his nose, humming as he stirs and whisks and creates appetising aromas, stopping to take a slurp of his beer from time to time and smacking his lips loudly.

Placing a large bowl of salad and another of potato mayonnaise on the table, he sits down, drinking beer and smoking his pipe, talking about his love of gardening and classical music. The time passes pleasantly. He sweats energetically, wiping his brow and upper lip with his sleeve every few minutes. His nose is huge and pendulous, and reminds me of a proboscis monkey. Swaying from its tip is a liquid drop that reflects the candlelight, like a crystal on a chandelier. I watch in fascination as it swings from side to side, elongates, and finally plops onto his lap. He glances down and rubs it with his cuff.

As we are finishing our first course - some delicate little cheese-pastry tartlets filled with a mushroom duxelles – he slaps three tuna steaks onto the barbecue where they sizzle fragrantly. Alice eats less than a sparrow, and certainly not bread, cheese or dessert, she explains, because she's been a size ten since she was twelve years old and hasn't any intention of changing that.

"The tuna is delicious, Dick," I say, "cooked to perfection."

He grunts, but looks pleased. "Not bad, although I still hold there's nothing to beat a good steak. Nice and bloody - preferably still alive," he chortles.

"Sometimes you're very coarse," Alice tells him, patting my hand and advising me to take no notice. Dick clears away all the dishes and then returns with a cheese board.

As he leans over to place it on the table, I look up and see another dewdrop, a stalactite descending from his cavernous nostril. It hangs tantalisingly over the cheese board, and I dare not breathe. A slight breeze comes from nowhere; the candles dance madly, a door slams, and the crystal drop detaches itself and plunges onto the board.

I decline the cheese, saying I am full. Then he brings a plate of fresh pineapple that he has chopped up and sprinkled with rum. Alice allows herself a meagre helping - fresh fruit isn't fattening, she explains - but I seem to have lost my appetite.

While Dick clears the table and tackles the washing up, Alice shares out the remaining wine with me. She looks at me over the rim of her glass, and says: "You don't like Dick. I've seen the way you look at him. And you wonder why somebody like me is with somebody like him."

I feel my face turn scarlet.

"I don't blame you," she goes on. "It's only for a few weeks a year, when we go on holiday together. I don't live with him. God forbid! But he has his uses; and that's all I'm going to say. Drink up, there's a drop more left."

This fortnight has passed quickly, and both couples are leaving today.

Ellen is tearful.

"I don't want to go," she wails. "I want to stay here."

James hugs her and, kissing her eyelids, reminds her of all the photos he has taken and promises they will come back next year. She hugs me, and James hugs me, and we all hug each other and shed a few tears, and they walk slowly to their hired car with handfuls of lavender and a plastic ice cream tub filled with raspberries.

They really have left Pissenlit immaculate, I am delighted to see. Every surface shines; the oven is spotless, likewise the bathroom, and the cushions are plumped up ready for the newcomers. Nothing for me to do except change the linen and refill the basket with goodies for the next arrivals. On the kitchen surface they have left behind a small plastic pot of black pepper and half a jar of strawberry jam, which I remove to the house.

Over the next few years almost every guest will leave behind half a jar of jam and a small plastic pot of black pepper, and although I briefly considered mixing all the left-over jam into fresh pots for incoming guests, I can't bring myself to do so. It would come in useful, though, when I needed to give one of the horses aspirin powder, which she would take more than willingly in a thick jam sandwich. The black pepper was tipped into ever larger containers, and I think we still have some left now.

Lavande is also spotless. I heard Alice at just after 7.00 am directing Dick to hoover under the bed settee, shake the rugs, clean the windows and oven, and load several boxes of empty bottles into their car. I know I shall not see them again. Alice has enjoyed her stay, but thinks next year they will probably go to Amalfi, where her daughter owns a very large and expensive villa. Before they go she reminds me to do something about the gravel and to keep my hair up because it will make my face look less plump. As well as the small plastic pot of black pepper and half jar of strawberry jam, they leave behind a number of rough patches on the stairs in the shape of delicate little footprints engrained with grit.

My next booking gets off on the wrong foot. A couple turned up – she's olive-skinned and petite with huge eyes, and he's blond and a bit rotund – I greet them at the gate, and show them into Pissenlit.

"Oh," says the petite lady when I take them up the stairs. "I thought there were two bedrooms, and it looked far larger on your website."

I make soothing, reassuring noises and leave them to unpack. Shortly she comes to say they're going shopping and will be back in an hour.

To remind myself of the names of the next guests for Lavande, I check the booking diary, and see that I've mixed people up and put the wrong couples in the wrong cottages. I dash into Pissenlit, grab all their clothes and bags, and move them into Lavande, and when they return apologise profusely. They're very gracious and good-natured, and pleased they are getting what they had paid for.

Then another car draws up, and out climb a gargantuan couple. They stand at the gate beaming.

"Hey, hey, we're the Hunters, but they call us the Bunters!" yells the woman. "He's Billy, I'm Bessy."

As they waddle towards Pissenlit, I'm trying to visualise them getting up the staircase, which is particularly narrow. They can barely squeeze through the front door, and once they're inside they occupy almost all the space.

"Lovely dovely! Smashing little place," says Bessy.

"I'll show you upstairs," I say.

"Going to be a tight fit," Bessy laughs as she puts a foot on the first stair. "Billy, you'll have to push."

And Billy does push, and heave, and Bessy drags herself up by the handrail, shrieking with laughter. Billy reaches the top of the stairs red-faced and panting and laughing too. They both plop down onto the bed, which I expect to crash through the floor.

"You're going to have to come down backwards, love," says Billy. "Otherwise you'll be pulled down by the force of gravity."

"You can talk," she replies. "You'll have to go down first and catch me if I fall."

Bessy bounces up and down on the bed.

"We're going to like it here, Billy."

"Bessy, you're right!"

33

When they laugh it's like watching two jellies during an earth tremor.

For the whole week I hear continuous sounds of merriment, even when two of the new plastic garden chairs splinter and collapse beneath them, leaving them helpless with mirth, laying flat on their backs like big pink turtles.

Chapter Five
Year One – The Nothingness of it All

MANY years ago when we used to stay in gîtes it was as much adventure as holiday. Then the word signified inexpensive rustic accommodation with no frills, elementary sanitation and electricity, and quite likely resident rodents. We had stayed at places where the beds were collapsed, the roof leaking, the plumbing archaic, the electricity lethal and the comfort minimal. And we had enjoyed every moment. The primitiveness lent an element of excitement. Having to flick the light switch with a piece of wood to avoid the risk of a shock; showering under a hose in the garden as an alternative to sitting in a scratchy old bath in rusty water; circumnavigating rotten floorboards painted with warning "X"s and trying to cook for crowds on a prehistoric oven. Lizards and beetles in the house, wasps, hornets and possibly snakes in the garden, and instructions as to where to position the buckets in the event of a storm were all part of the fun and romance of our holiday.

Things have changed since then. Newcomers have arrived with bulging bank accounts courtesy of soaring property values in England. They have bought up farmhouses with outbuildings and converted them into luxury holiday complexes with central heating, swimming pools, jacuzzis, satellite TV, home cinemas, inclusive use of cars, motorbikes and boats.

Our two cottages are simple and comfortable, weatherproof and (fairly) safe, designed for short breaks for people seeking to escape from the maddened crowd, opt out of the rat race, and relax. We provide French TV and radio, a CD player and a stack of books and board games. We are 80 miles from the sea but there is a park and swimming lake with beach just three miles away. We're 25 miles from any retail therapy opportunities, and I've no idea where the nearest boîte de nuit (night club) is to be found. Guests are advised accordingly: Don't arrive here expecting a rave; think "chilled out."

The neighbours are baffled as to why we have spent money on two ruins when we have an almost-habitable house. The house was a virtual ruin when we bought it. Over the last few years we've been gradually renovating it, but it's still fairly primitive by most people's standards. One bemused old lady asks, "Who is going to come here?"

I explain that holidaymakers will come for one or two weeks at a time, during the summer months.

"But why would anybody want to come here? It's so quiet; there's nothing to see, and nothing to do."

In our 12-house hamlet the most exciting event has hitherto been the sighting of a lost dog from the chasse, or the arrival of the swallows. The older residents mourn distant days when it was a lively farming community, and from dawn to dusk every day of the year the sounds of chatter, livestock and machinery filled the air. Now, they say sadly, it's all too quiet. Life is boring. Nothing happens.

I tell her that it is that nothingness that attracts city people. The lack of ambient light at night, showing the stars in their full brilliance; the absence of man-made noise, allowing us to enjoy nature's sounds; the lack of traffic on the roads, and the lack of parking meters and struggles to find somewhere to leave the car when we go shopping. The lack of notices threatening fines for the smallest demeanour. The lack of CCTV cameras. The absence of feral youths. The freedom to walk through fields and the absence of "Private Property" notices. In fact there is one in our hamlet - it has been hand-painted on a bit of board and wired to the gate of an English residence. It is a cause of great hilarity, and everybody assumes that it's meant to be an example of Anglo-Saxon humour.

People will come to stay here to enjoy the quiet open spaces, reliable summer weather, peace and quiet, wine and food, and the slow pace of life. For those who spend too much of their busy lives in stagnant traffic or on unreliable public transport, doing jobs they don't enjoy to earn money to buy things they don't need, a few days in this unspoiled countryside is a tonic. She looks as if she cannot imagine that people anywhere could really be living lives such as I have described. But as our summer visitors begin arriving our neighbours are rather pleased and proud that they live not, as they had believed, in a place of no consequence, but on the contrary, somewhere that sophisticated people actually pay to come and stay, and they are entertained by their comings and goings. The arrival of a new family brings faces to the windows, and summer days are suddenly more interesting. Children ride bikes up and down the lane. Adults play games of boules on the path - sometimes the neighbours are persuaded to join in. It's a novel source of entertainment.

Both the cottages are close to our house, and although each has its own private courtyard area, we are all within sight of each other. Some people like to keep to themselves, but most enjoy chatting and sharing an occasional drink and sometimes a meal. Several couples have formed friendships with their neighbours. They are all keen to know more about the history of the area, for advice on what to see and where to go while they're here. I have been asked to deal with a few spiders, lizards, a colony of ants, a funny noise (it turned out to be a bluebottle trapped in a spider's web) and a large toad that determinedly flops into the kitchen of Lavande whenever it has the opportunity. I'm on hand when they need me, and keep myself and the dogs out of the way unless we're invited. Most guests are animal lovers, and the cats take full advantage of the situation to supplement their diet with whatever they can by means of piteous meowing or brazen theft. Some people like to "borrow" the dogs – we have four gun dogs, one small terrier and Dolly, a blind part-Beagle - taking them for walks and otherwise entertaining them. The dogs are in seventh heaven.

There are guests who arrive with bulging suitcases and enjoy dressing up every day – the women fully-made up and beautifully manicured. Others live in shorts, T-shirts and flip-flops. Some like to dine out every night at different restaurants, and others are happy to stay in and eat al fresco.

While some visitors prefer to buy everything locally when they arrive, others bring those items they can't live without – mostly English bacon, Marmite, marmalade and Tetley tea bags. And when they leave, there is sometimes not a crumb to be seen, and other times the cupboards and fridge are full of unopened groceries. So far the nearest we've had to a complaint is the difficulty in finding fresh milk – it is available in limited quantities in the local supermarkets, but sells out quickly, so people have to buy

UHT. I've never been able to tell the difference, myself, but then I'm not a milk connoisseur.

Lavande's two double bedrooms and convertible bed settee can sleep six people comfortably, and the courtyard garden enjoys the sun from dawn until nightfall. However, it is impractical to heat during the colder months, so we close it in mid-October. But a wood-burning stove in one-up, one-down Pissenlit keeps it cosy even through the coldest months. The little place has other advantages, too. There are plenty of larger properties for rent, while economical places for a couple or singleton are quite rare, and we have bookings for Pissenlit from mid-March through to the end of December. The one drawback is the height of the doorway and beams, an inconvenient 5ft 5in (1.6 metres). That's just fine for real shorties who can pass beneath them unscathed, or for 6ft (1.8 metre) plus types who cannot avoid noticing them. It's the in-betweeners who regularly clout themselves. I've decorated the beams with brightly coloured objects, hung chimes from them, stuck rubber to their edges and placed strategic warnings, but still people thump into them and stagger around clutching their heads. I've put a large packet of sticking plasters in the First Aid box, and have to replace it fairly frequently.

Some guests don't know, and never ask, the meaning of Pissenlit, but those who do, or who ask, are always amused. The English name for a dandelion comes from the French "dent de lion" meaning lion's tooth, referring to the shape of the dandelion's leaves, but in France it's called the "pissenlit," which means "piss in the bed." It was a bit risqué naming it thus, but that's my quirky sense of humour coming out. Nobody so far has been offended

39

or upset. And nobody has taken it as either an order or invitation, yet.

Chapter Six
Year One – Could Be Cleaner

WHEN I had told Carole, a long-standing and outspoken friend, that we were converting the two buildings into holiday accommodation, she'd expressed doubts about the project.

"Have you thought what it's going to be like, having strangers all over your property for the entire summer? What if you get some really awful people? You'll be stuck with them."

I couldn't see that awful people would want to come to this quiet part of the world, and if they did, tant pis, it would only be for a week or so. They weren't going to become full-time neighbours and we didn't have to become bosom friends.

"Then there's the cleaning," Carole went on. "You're going to have to clean the places thoroughly before every new guest arrives. They'll have to be spotless."

Breezily, I'd replied: "They will be, because the outgoing guests will clean before they leave." I believed that.

"I hope you're right, but I think you're being very optimistic."

"Well, maybe one or two might leave a bit of a mess, but I'll be able to cope with that." I believed that too.

Carole pulled a little face and raised her eyebrows. "Are you sure? No offence, but housework never has been your strongest point."

She was quite right. I'm hopeless. Still, I thought she was worrying needlessly. With all the necessary cloths, cleaning materials, brushes and a vacuum cleaner in both cottages, I can't see any reason why people shouldn't clean up before they leave. I've been trusting and relying on them to do so. All I do before new guests arrive is to make the beds, check the loos, and give the baths and basins a wipe down. It doesn't take more than an hour to finish both places, and it looks absolutely fine.

Therefore I am rocked to my foundations reading the guest book one hot Saturday when I go to do the changeover.

"Pleasant part of the world, weather has been fantastic. Nice friendly welcome, enjoyed the wildlife and wine. Place could have been a bit cleaner, though."

Cleaner? It was immaculate. I rip the page out of the book, and phone Carole to let off steam.

"I'll drop in on my way by and have a look," she says.

When she arrives she wanders around Pissenlit for a few minutes, making little tutty noises.

"Have you seen this?"

She points into the fridge, and I notice some grey-green spots on the rubber seal. There are loose peas and something pink and sticky has oozed all over the bottom of the freezer compartment.

"Um," I say.

"For heaven's sake, you mean you haven't given them a proper clean since you opened?"

"Not really. They looked clean," I reply, lamely.

I trail around with her despondently as she points out that the hob is sticky, the bath has a faint grey rim around it that I hadn't noticed, and the underside of the loo seat is not clean. There are cobwebs in the corners and hanging from the beams. Clouds of sluts' wool snuggle beneath the beds. One of the bedside tables has several rings of wine stains. There are small crusts of dried food on some of the cutlery, and the crockery is greasy underneath. Carole holds up glasses to the light, revealing fingerprints, smudges, lipstick. Lavande is much the same.

"Oh dear," she says.

"Oh dear," I repeat. "That's very strange. It all looked perfectly clean to me."

After our first guests, the six boys, had left everything so clean and tidy, I had truly imagined that everybody else had done so as well. Now I realise that what they have been doing is at best only a superficial job.

"Well, you're lucky you haven't had more complaints," Carole says. "You are going to have to check more carefully in future. This isn't just one family not cleaning up. It's taken weeks to get to this state."

I am renowned for my lack of domestic skills. The prospect of having to clean floors, windows, ovens and baths makes me break into a sweat. I love cooking, which I do erratically, will happily iron flat things for several hours, but I loathe cleaning. There is some deep psychological hang-up which causes me immense stress when faced with a vacuum cleaner, duster and cleaning products. My heartbeat increases, my head starts to spin, I feel panicky and totally incompetent. Maybe it dates back to earlier life in Kenya. Our house servant, apart from cooking like a dream and doing all the laundry, cheerfully and apparently effortlessly maintained an immaculately clean house with nothing more than a packet of Omo, a bucket, scrubbing brush and handful of cloths. And this was despite four dogs, a cat, two small children and countless visitors. I could never hope to emulate him. Until I was in my mid-twenties and left Kenya, I had never done any housework at all, and I don't seem to have ever been able to get the knack.

After Carole has gone, I stare gloomily into space listening to the minutes ticking away towards the arrival of new guests, trying to summon up the motivation to start cleaning. The longer I delay the worse it gets, but I cannot get going. The sound of a car engine approaching sends me into full panic mode. Somebody is three hours early. I put on my polite-but-exasperated face, ready to firmly but nicely send them away until 4.00 pm, the agreed check-in time.

But there's a pleasant surprise – it's Tristram delivering a dozen geraniums that Beverly has raised from cuttings. The children spill around our ankles; our dogs would like to socialise with them, but the Dachsies are independent and aloof little creatures and ignore all approaches, snuffling busily around in nooks and crannies like health inspectors looking for bacteria.

Absent-mindedly I make a pot of mint tea, forgetting to remove the stalk and roots from the mint.

"Are you OK? You look a bit, well, stricken," says Tristram. "As if something quite dreadful has happened." He tips away the tea and makes a new pot.

"It has." As I explain about the dirty cottages, ridiculously, pathetically, I begin to cry.

"I can't cope. I just cannot face cleaning two places every week - it makes me ill thinking about it. What am I going to do?"

He pulls a face, and says, "You'll just have to get on with it, my dear. It's only a few hours once a week, for a few weeks. It isn't that big a job. And it's not as if you're looking at a lifetime of domestic drudgery."

It is to me.

"Come on, I'll give you a hand."

He gives me a lesson in house cleaning, wiping down surfaces, knocking cobwebs from the ceiling, lifting the cushions off the chairs and brushing out the accumulated detritus – we find coins, sweets, crumbs and a hard-core porn magazine. We vacuum beneath all the furniture before passing a damp cloth over the floors.

"When you clean the surfaces and floor, put a drop of bleach in the water – it makes everything smell fresh and clean. Tip some down the plug-holes, too."

If I work methodically, he says, even in the worst case it shouldn't take longer than an hour to clean each cottage. Between us we finish long before the new guests arrive, and again I bless the day I met Tristram.

The cleaning really doesn't seem that difficult and I can't understand why I make so much fuss about it, but I am still utterly depressed at the thought of having to do this every time guests leave. It's bad enough having to do my own house, let alone another two.

The following Saturday I put my new-found domestic skills to the test, remembering all those places that Carole had told me to check, and wiping down everywhere with a bleach-soaked cloth. It isn't that arduous, except for the half hour spent dismantling and unblocking the vacuum cleaner of a sweet wrapper and a long wodge of compacted fluff. I think that with a bit of backbone and positive attitude I can probably cope for the few remaining weeks of the season. I make sure everywhere is properly cleaned, even the microwaves and ovens, and after a couple of weeks have convinced myself that I've been making a fuss about nothing.

Chapter Seven
Year One – Wallbangers and Others

PISSENLIT'S current occupants are a pair of medical students in their twenties: Matt has the physique and rather battered face of a rugby player. Elaine is thin and pale with crinkly red hair. When they arrived Matt returned the bottle of wine from the welcome pack, explaining that they are teetotallers. Not your archetypal medical students then. They're not a very lively pair, sitting all day drinking tea, munching biscuits and studying text books.

Jenny comes round this afternoon and we take the dogs for a walk through the sunflower fields. When we pass Matt and Elaine they are sitting demurely in their small courtyard reading, the teapot on the table. About half a mile down the road I remember I have forgotten to take the bread out of the oven so I sprint back towards the house. As I round the corner into the courtyard I hear a rhythmic, grunting, moaning and gasping. In the fraction of a second before I turn my head away, I cannot help noticing a muscular pair of frantically pumping male buttocks. Matt has Elaine pinned to the wall of the courtyard and he seems to be trying to hammer her into it. They are both wearing their shorts around their ankles, and her head and hands are smothered in the Virginia creeper. Matt's chin is hooked over Elaine's shoulder, her face buried within the foliage. I continue running into the house. Whether the crunchy gravel noise is drowned out by their own noise, or whether they are too engrossed to notice me, I don't know.

Having removed the bread from the oven, I wonder how long to wait before venturing out again. There's no way out other than passing them. Soon Jenny is going to wonder what has happened if I don't reappear. I faff around in the house for five minutes, humming, talking to myself and generally being noisy to signal that I am not likely to appear imminently. After holding an imaginary telephone conversation in a loud voice, I shout: "Cheerio! I'm off out now." Then I bang a couple of doors and, chirping to the parrot "See you later," I amble out of the house, past the courtyard where Matt and Elaine are sitting at the table, with their pile of books, teapot and a packet of Garibaldi biscuits. They glance up and nod and smile as I trot past. Do they know I saw them, or not?

When they leave at the end of the week, I laugh aloud at what they have written in the guest book:

"A wonderful stay in adorable little Pissenlit. Thank you for your hospitality and for making us so welcome. We have thoroughly enjoyed our visit and meeting you and all your animals. It has been a perfect relaxing holiday, with plenty of fresh air, and just what we needed."

They have drawn a smiley face, and signed: "The Harvey Wallbangers."

The next guests are a sophisticated couple from the Home Counties who spend their days visiting vineyards to stock their cellars – the Haut Poitou wines are becoming increasingly popular. Every evening they invite me to sample the wines they have bought that day, and to play a few rounds of Scrabble. Rosemary is the regional champion of her county in England, and she has brought the Official Scrabble Dictionary with her. She doesn't like to lose, and after my second visit I make certain not to win – which is sometimes an interesting challenge as the Fates seem to be dealing me all the high-value tiles and necessary vowels to make great scores. I try to play as ineptly as possible. It's rather like trying to ride a bicycle backwards, I imagine.

Two elderly couples are sharing Lavande, long-standing friends whose passion is religious architecture. They are all scholarly, but at the same time very jolly, and tell me that this area is a veritable treasure chest of delights. The gloomy little village church, the startling décor of the Romanesque church in our nearest town, the splendour of the frescoes at the abbey at St Savin - a UNESCO World Heritage site - and the 4th century Baptistery in Poitiers are all jewels to add to their collection.

From piles of books and maps they plan each day's excursions with precision, and very kindly invite me to join them for a visit to the fortified abbey at Nouaillé Maupertuis. It's a stunning medieval building, not far from the battlefield where Edward the Black Prince defeated and captured the French king Jean le Bon at the battle of Poitiers in 1356. With a moat, a medicinal herb garden, a row of tiny cottages, turrets with arrow slots and cobbled alleyways, Nouaillé Maupertuis is both imposing and quaint.

Our little party examine every stone, every feature, and talk in hushed, excited tones in a language as foreign to me as Japanese. I am reminded how fortunate we are to live in a part of the world where people come hundreds of miles to admire the various attractions to which we have become blasé and take for granted. We picnic beside the herb garden. While they discuss squinches, pendentives and dosserets I nod wisely. They've brought a heavenly spread for our picnic – a lobster terrine, crispy salad, great selection of cheeses, and a box of exquisite petit fours. Two bottles of Sancerre, and a bottle of champagne, plus a bottle of apricot liqueur to mix with the champagne. By the time we've scraped up the last morsel and squeezed the bottles dry, we subside one by one and fall asleep on the grass, waking only when the early evening shadows drape themselves over us.

Pissenlit's latest guests are a bit odd, a couple in their early thirties, slender and rather aloof. They dress identically and are very similar in appearance. Daytime wear is always beige trousers, loafers, crisp white shirts and wide-brimmed straw hats. Like something from the set of Out of Africa. In the evenings they both wear white. His hair is gelled, the front twisted up into a little curly wave and he smokes through a cigarette holder. She plasters her hair onto her face like a film star from the old silent screen. I don't know if they are brother and sister, or husband and wife, but I have found them particularly irritating. They've complained about spiders, flies, crickets and lizards, the noise of frogs croaking and the fridge humming, and finding ants walking across the path. Fingers crossed they don't see the bats, or the grass snakes that live in the pond.

The girl makes a great deal of fuss when she sees our dogs, who normally don't approach anybody unless invited to do so. They are used to people coming and going. Every time she passes the courtyard coming in or going out, she squeals, yelps and flaps her hands round her ears, shouting "Oh Sweet Jesus, don't let them jump on me! They'll ruin my clothes." The squealing, yelping and flapping interests the dogs, who go to investigate, sending her into near hysterics and ever wilder arm flailing. Despite my assurance that if she ignores them and doesn't flail her arms around noisily they will ignore her, she continues to do so, so I've confined them in our back garden until she leaves. In the evenings, when she's had a few drinks she leans over the gate, feeds them paper napkins and jumps around trying to make them dance. The poor dogs don't know what they are meant to do, and I'll be glad when this couple have gone.

A gleaming black 4x4 with tinted windows and a robust roof rack holding two canoes and two bicycles rolls up to the gate and hoots. A loud man jumps out and stands with his head thrown back, swinging his arms across his chest, crying "Ah YES!"

He runs round to the passenger side and yanks open the door, shouting "Let's be having you, young man!"

A young blonde boy slowly climbs down from the car, and stands looking around. Both men are dressed in camouflage jackets and trousers, black boots and green vests. With the temperature 36°C (96°F) in the shade, they must be feeling pretty warm. The older man is tanned, he wears a webbing belt with a sheath attached to it, and what looks like a compass strapped to his wrist. The boy is paler and stands with his arms hanging at his sides.

I go to the gate to welcome them.

"Ho!" cries the tanned man. "We've found you!"

"Ho!" I reply. "Welcome."

He grabs my hand in both of his, and pumps it up and down for a moment. "Malc," he says, "and the son and heir, Steven. We've brought him out for a break. A boys-only holiday. Toughen him up."

He punches the boy's shoulder affectionately.

"Don't be shy! Say 'hello'."

Steven holds out his hand obediently.

"How nice to meet you," he says politely. He has a very direct gaze and calm grey eyes, and his father's wide smile.

"Put her down! Going to be a ladies' man, just like his old dad, aren't you?"

He jabs a playful elbow into Steven's shoulder. "Come on son, let's get unloaded, then we'll cook ourselves a meal."

Steven knocks on my door a little later.

"Excuse me, my father wants to know if it would be alright for us to make a fire in the garden?"

"A fire? What for?"

"We're going to cook steaks."

I say, "There's a barbecue on the patio. And plenty of charcoal. Just help yourselves."

"Yes, I know, but my father wants us to build our own fire." His eyes and voice are embarrassed.

"It's not a good time to light fires outside. It's very dry. But I suppose it will be OK if he lights it in the corner where the gravel is, as long as you watch it really carefully and make sure you put it out afterwards."

"Oh, we will. Thanks very much. He knows what he's doing, so no worries."

Then they come to ask if they can go into the field to collect wood, and come back with an armful of twigs and branches. I don't want to spoil their fun, but am quite concerned that they might burn the whole place down, so I sit in the garden with a drink and book and watch them surreptitiously through a gap in the hedge. Malc sends Steven to collect some largish stones, which he lays out in a small circle, then sets the wood inside it. Smoke begins to rise. I hear Malc showing Steven how to put potatoes into the fire to bake, and later how to thread steak onto skewers to cook. Their voices are low and pleasant, and they finish their starlit meal with coffee made over the fire. One of them plays a guitar, quietly, for half an hour. I fully expect them to ask to borrow saddles and then roll up in blankets and sleep on the lawn. Before I go to bed I check to make sure that Malc has put out the fire. I think to myself how pleasing it is to see father and son so close to each other.

Malc is an early riser. "Hands off cocks and on with socks!" His voice carries through the open windows at 7.00 am every day. Once he's risen he doesn't settle until late. He has worked out a busy schedule for Steven's toughening up, and before breakfast they have a five-mile jog and do 50 push-ups. Then they're off to take full advantage of the local sporting activities - kayaking, fishing, swimming, horse-riding, cross-country cycling, archery, and an arboreal activity centre he has heard about where you can clamber about and swing in trees. Every day they have to do something manly. From Steven's very quiet behaviour, I don't think he's that keen on all these activities, and thankfully Malc either doesn't know about, or has ruled out, the bungee jumping from a viaduct half an hour away.

When they return from these expeditions their day is far from over. Before the nightly meal around the camp fire, Steven has to continue his toughening up. Malc asks whether I have any logs that need chopping or trees that need felling.

"The lad would love to be useful."

They kick a football backwards and forwards, and arm-wrestle. Malc is always shouting at Steven to "put his back into it!" He has also several times yelled out that it's time for Steven to "get his winkle wet."

My feelings towards Malc are ambivalent. He's very full of himself, and has been everywhere anyone else has been, but further. He's done everything anyone else has done, but better. He has an encyclopaedic knowledge of everything about himself, and he's totally insensitive to the fact that his son isn't particularly enjoying himself. But he obviously worships the boy and believes he's giving him a good time. He's devoting all his energy to entertaining him. The sad thing is that he's trying to make Steven into something he doesn't want to be, and almost certainly never will be.

While Steven is out one evening collecting firewood, Malc confides that he is very worried about his son. He feels that Steven's masculine side is not developing because he lives with his mother. He hopes that he'll join the army.

Steven wants to study art, like his mother, and seems to have a talent for it. He's shown me a few sketches he's made of our dogs, and a couple of landscapes, and to my admittedly untrained eye they are very impressive. But any time he sits down his father urges him to get up and "be active." He's a boy any parent would be proud of, and sometimes I can see that he is mortified, yet he deals with his father's crass behaviour with good humour. It's almost a role reversal, with the teenager the tolerant parent of an uncouth offspring.

For their last night Malc decides they will take his Bowie knife, a torch and a tarpaulin, and spend the night in the wild, hoping to kill something which they can cook on a pointed stick over a fire. I scotch that idea by telling him, completely untruthfully, that the local farmers are aggressive, suspicious and extremely territorial, and that they shoot first and ask no questions. Furthermore, and this is true, it is illegal to light a fire in the fields during the summer, and if the gendarmes catch him he'll be thrown into an oubliette. So instead they have their last evening meal around the campfire in the garden, and are up at sunrise to clear away any trace. To their credit, they have left the place immaculate.

When I say goodbye, I am torn between hugging Malc and smacking him and telling him to calm down and let his son be what he wants to be. I feel really quite sad that he doesn't realise just what a lovely child he has and appreciate him as he is.

While he is loading the car, I chat to Steven for a few moments, and wish him well. He says they're off to spend a week in the Gorges du Tarn, where they will go white water rafting, caving, and rock climbing. I give him a little hug and tell him to enjoy himself. He gives a wry smile. "I'll do my best. It makes Dad happy."

Chapter Eight
Year One – Cold Anger

IF I had to nominate my favourite month of the year, it would be September. I've always loved autumn with its rich colours, the departure of the bluebottles, the peace that lies over the countryside, the collecting of walnuts and grapes, and pleasantly warm days and cool evenings with a whiff of woodsmoke on the air. When we had an enquiry early in the year from a couple who would be coming with a very young baby as to what the weather would be like during the first week of September, without any hesitation I had forecast that it would be ideal. Warm enough for the baby to be out in the garden during the day without risk of burning, and still cosy at night. This year hasn't been remarkable for good weather. We've had quite a few rainy days and temperatures have been on the low side. One of our neighbours said that some time during the 1960s the summer had been so cold that they'd had snow in July, but I thought he was exaggerating. But during the last week of August it really has started to get very cold, and I am wearing woollies and having to light a fire every night.

It is irrational, but whenever the weather is disappointing I always feel guilty and personally responsible as if I have failed in a moral obligation to my guests. The forecast for the coming days doesn't indicate any improvement in the temperatures, so I write to warn the new parents to bring plenty of warm clothing for themselves and their baby, given that there is no heating in Lavande. There's no response, so I write again, twice, stressing that it is really very cold indeed, and receive a brief reply to the effect that they have taken notice of my advice.

They arrive in watery sunshine, wearing T-shirts and shorts, and as soon as they get out of the car they are shivering. She has a thin, angry face and snaps commands at her husband, who is kindly and gentle with her. I take them into Lavande, and show them the brand new cot I have bought for their baby, (it has cost more than half the week's rental, but I suppose that it will come in useful in the future), with a safety mattress and cover, and a jolly little musical mobile clipped to it. She makes no comment, and there is an awkward silence and tense feeling in the air. I've put two thick wool blankets on the end of their bed to supplement the summer duvet, and ask them to let me know if there's anything they need. Ten minutes later she is hammering at the door, still wearing a T-shirt and shorts, white-faced and tight-lipped, arms wrapped around her chest, asking why the heating hasn't been switched on. I remind her politely that there is no heating, which is clearly stated on our website, and that I had emailed her three times to let her know how cold the weather was. I haven't often met anybody quite so furious or quite so rude. While she shrieks a tirade of threats about "trade descriptions" I remain polite and outwardly calm. What I try to remember, even on those rare occasions when we have particularly objectionable guests, is that they have paid me to enjoy themselves, and I must do whatever is within my power to make sure they do. Sometimes I can make a difference, and sometimes I can't, but my cardinal rule is that I will always be as pleasant and as helpful as I possibly can.

When the angry woman temporarily runs out of breath and invective, I remind her again that I had warned them before they came, and suggest that they put on warmer clothing. They didn't BRING warmer clothing, she replies. When I had written that it was cold, they didn't believe it could be THAT cold. On the Internet it said that the temperature in September should be about 20° Celsius. Yes, it should, but it isn't this year. I'm no happier about it than she is, but I have no control over the weather. The best I can do is to lend them some jumpers and my paraffin heater. She sends her husband to collect the heater. He looks thoroughly haggard, poor man. He has changed into a fascinating pair of jeans. They are obviously home-made, and the seams are askew so that they start at the sides but curl around his long skinny legs and end up pointing at his toes.

He tells me that their holiday is a combined anniversary and birthday present for her, and that the next day they are going to Futuroscope. Inwardly I shudder. I can't imagine anything much worse than trudging around in the awful weather, with the baby, who will prevent them from going into the dynamic cinemas and probably scream from the noise of the other non-dynamic cinemas, but I don't want to be the messenger of doom, so I tell him about the translation headphones, draw a map from here to there, and advise them to wear comfortable shoes because there's a lot of walking to be done.

Even with the windows closed, I can hear the baby crying several times during the night. I don't think we've ever had unhappier guests. Thankfully the guests in Pissenlit are a merry Irish couple in their late 70s, who are not in the least dismayed by the cold. They've come for ten days, equipped with warm and waterproof clothing and walking boots, and set off cheerfully every morning to explore the countryside. Every evening they dress up and go to try out the local restaurants, and as far as they are concerned, they're having a wonderful time here. Before they leave, they bring me a box of chocolates and a bottle of champagne. They know how stressed I am feeling about the cold guests, but they say I must be philosophical. "You can please some people all the time, all of the people some of the time, but never all the people all the time. Bringing a tiny baby all this way, well, did they not think that was rather foolish? You couldn't do any more than you've already done, so stop worrying about it." They write in the guest book: 'go n-éirí an t-ádh libh'. It means, I learn, "May you succeed really well."

Whatever else, I can't succeed in pleasing Lavande's guests. The windows are running with condensation. The day after their visit to Futuroscope I knock on the door to ask if they are alright. She opens the door a meagre crack and glares silently.

"Good morning," I sing brightly. "Did you enjoy your trip yesterday? She looks as if she'd like to scratch out my eyes. He looms over her shoulder.

"It was a bit of a disappointment, in fact. We only managed to see three of the cinemas, because we couldn't go in to some of them with the baby. And he cried a lot, too. So it was not quite what we were hoping for."

I murmur something about being sorry to hear that.

"Bloody waste of time and money, thank you. So not only are we frozen, we can't enjoy ourselves because of the bloody baby. I wish we didn't have the damned thing. And I wish we hadn't come here." She has tears in her eyes, and that's when I realise that she's probably suffering from post-natal depression. She pushes the door closed.

Their car drives away a little later, and they haven't returned by the time I go to bed at midnight. I wonder if they've had an accident somewhere? Where can they be with such a small baby, on such a cold night? Or have they packed up and gone home? I can't sleep and keep getting up to see if there are any lights on. The car is still not back at 2.30 am. I'm worried sick.

However, next morning their car is parked outside, and looks undamaged. He is walking up and down with the baby in his arms, and she's standing in the doorway wrapped in a duvet. "I'm glad to see you! I was a bit worried when you weren't back last night," I say. That's a mistake.

"Please forgive us," she says sarcastically. "We didn't know that we had to report our movements to you."

I give up then, and leave them to themselves. When they leave they do nothing to clean up behind them. The place is a mess, and there's a bulging and aromatic sack of used disposable nappies in the kitchen. There are three fan heaters plugged in and still running at full speed. A few months later, I will find that our electricity bill for the period covering their stay is more than the cost of the rent they paid. They have not left a message in the guest book, but she emails the following week to say it was the most miserable holiday she had ever had, and she had a good mind to write to the BBC about it.

Our friends Ellie and Robert also have two holiday cottages, but not on their property, and as a result they barely know any of their guests. Almost the only time they ever hear from them is if something goes wrong, which, they say, is fairly frequently. They confess that although initially they thought we would find people living so close to us an unwelcome intrusion, they are now envious of the fact that each week brings new people to our door, and all of them are interesting in one way or another. Percentage-wise, they estimate that one in four of their guests is either unhappy or difficult about something or other. When I calculate our happy to unhappy client ratio it works out at ten to one, which they think is extraordinary, but it still irks me. I want everybody to be happy and satisfied. One hundred percent. Unrealistic, they say. It's all about human nature. There are some people who will always complain about nothing and everything, just as there are people who will always make the best of the best and worst of things.

Three of this year's guests have already booked for next year, so I should be happy. But the vision of that screaming baby, drained woman, defeated-looking husband and the tear-stained windows stay with me for weeks.

By the middle of October the holiday season is over, and I do a final clean of both cottages and throw dust covers over everything until next year.

Then in November an enquiry arrives from a couple who want to book Pissenlit for three months. They are returning to England after an extended holiday in the US, and their dog needs to live in Europe for six months to qualify for a canine passport to allow it into England. They plan to stay three months enjoying rural France, and then either extend their stay, or move to another region.

Chapter Nine
Year One – The Hollywooders

THEY arrive in mid-December, Samantha and Jay, both born in Hollywood, with their greyhound Thomas, who came from Battersea Dogs' Home. Jay and Samantha have written that they are hardy creatures, but Thomas feels the cold, so I've had the wood stove in Pissenlit going for a couple of days to warm the place, stockpiled a supply of logs, and put an electric blanket on the bed. At present the weather is fine, clear skies and plenty of sunshine, but there are hard frosts each morning and the temperature is down below zero at night. Coming from Hollywood at this time of year, into a French winter, I hope they are prepared. But I have some misgivings.

Thomas, a large beige-coloured greyhound with unbearably sad eyes is shivering despite wearing a heavy red coat with a sheepskin collar. While Jay is an average-looking man with glossy black hair and a hearty handshake, Samantha is something to behold. Six foot three, with naturally blonde wavy hair down to the small of her back, perfect teeth, perfect skin, a huge smile and the longest legs I've seen except on a racehorse. She is a stunningly beautiful woman. Looking at them, as they stand by the gate, I cannot imagine them all fitting into bijou little Pissenlit. For a start, there's Thomas's bed, a vast tartan padded nest with a thick fluffy mattress and several cushions. There is a 50 lb. sack of his special food, and a rucksack containing his toys. His drinking bowl and food bowl are both 18" in diameter, and fit onto a metal rack to keep them off the ground so he doesn't have to bend down to them. Then there are Samantha and Jay's six suitcases, plus a number of plastic shopping bags. As we trail from the car to the cottage heaving all this luggage, my heart sinks.

The first priority is to settle Thomas comfortably. His nest, which occupies almost one-quarter of the available floor space, is laid as close as possible to the stove, his toys lined up around it, and his food and water bowls filled. He climbs into his bed, tucks his sad face beneath his bony tail, and closes his eyes with a loud sigh.

If Jay was half an inch shorter he would not hit his head on the beams. Samantha has to bend her knees and stoop like an aged crone to pass beneath them. Upright, her head only just clears the ceiling. Gulliver must have felt like that during his stay in Lilliput.

Jay hauls their cases and bags up the stairs, leaving just sufficient floor space for Samantha and myself. I don't know what to say, but Samantha is a good sport, and laughs.

"Well, it's kinda smaller than I thought, but it's cosy. Thomas is happy. We're gonna be just fine."

When I suggest a cup of tea, Jay burrows in one of the plastic bags and withdraws six cans of beer.

"Forget the tea. Let's celebrate!" he cries, so we huddle together and soon the cans are empty and Samantha says Thomas needs a walk. First she puts a waterproof coat on top of his woollen one, and then his lead. He seems disinclined to leave his warm bed, but Samantha coaxes and cajoles, and with his tail clamped tight to his belly he reluctantly follows us down the lane to the vast fields behind the hamlet. Here a greyhound can safely run to his heart's content. When we reach the field Jay and

Samantha are thrilled at the sight of the wide open countryside and the fact that there is not a soul to be seen. Hollywood, they say, is hell.

Samantha throws Thomas's ball for him, and lopes down the path at a slow canter slapping her thigh and clicking her fingers, but Thomas just stands trembling morosely. All he wants to do is return to his bed.

"He's probably jet-lagged," she says, as he tows her back to the cottage.

I show Jay how to stock up the stove from the log pile, and he finds that if he walks around in his socks he can just scrape beneath the beam without braining himself. Perhaps they'd like to come in for a meal this evening, I suggest. They accept eagerly. I think Sam will enjoy being able to walk around upright for a few hours. Thomas does not come with them; he is nervous of our dogs and prefers to stay in his bed by the fire.

Despite having just flown across the Atlantic and driven straight down here from Paris, they are both lively, wide-awake, and amusing company. Jay talks almost non-stop, in a smooth drawl, while Sam's voice, when she can get a word in, is deep and husky. He's a school teacher and she works for the National Health Service. In Hollywood she had been a leg model and Jay had his own successful business. They had a beautiful home and a high standard of living, but, said Sam, felt a need to change their lifestyle and so emigrated to London ten years ago. Although he is American by birth, Jay tells people that he's German, having spent his childhood there. Sam refers to herself as a Londoner. Now that they have Thomas, they need to move from their flat and buy a house with a garden, which is why they had taken a trip to the States to see their families before they have to "work their butts off to repay the bank."

For a teacher, Jay has an unusual attitude towards children. He hates them. What the little bastards need, he says, is the lash. Good and hard. Because that's all they respect. Given his way, he'd start their day with a routine flogging. He has twice found himself barricaded into a second floor classroom with a number of other teachers repelling an assault by several dozen "feral youths". Sam doesn't stand for any nonsense. When she saw a teenage yob in London terrorising elderly people on the street with a pump-action water pistol, she had grabbed it from him, jumped on it, then picked him up by the head and shaken him. The yob had taken to his heels to the applause of onlookers. Don't mess with this couple.

Despite their rather violent tendencies they are a really gentle and compassionate pair, whose interests are human rights and animal welfare, and I like them very much.

Next day they surface late morning, having slept for twelve hours. They haven't been able to relight the fire, which has gone out overnight. The floor is strewn with spent matches and singed pieces of newspaper. This is their first experience of heating that is not activated by a simple switch, and they are finding it a struggle. I show Jay how to lay the kindling and fire-lighter, and get it going for them. Thomas is shivering despite his thick red coat and the fluffy blanket in his tartan bed. While he is well-equipped for the weather, the same cannot be said of Sam and Jay. Apart from jeans and T-shirts, they have between them one very large khaki jumper full of holes, and a black and white herringbone patterned winter coat. They have decided to walk to the village a mile away, taking Thomas with them, to enjoy a coffee. Jay wears the jumper, Samantha the coat, whose cuffs end mid-way between her wrists and elbows.

They return an hour later, shell-shocked.

"Did we go to the right place?" asks Jay.

I point in the general direction, and say "Just down there. A mile away."

"Yeah. You mean that's it? Just that small place?"

"Well yes. Just the bakery and the café, and the little general store. That's all there is."

"Oh jeez," moans Jay. "I can't believe that. We were expecting something quaint."

Although it has its own charm, quaint is not an adjective that can be honestly applied to our nearest village.

"Didn't you read what it says on our website? That there is just a church, a bakery/grocery and a café?" I ask rather defensively.

"Yeah, sure, but we thought there would be a few little shops as well. There was nobody else in the café, and nothing to eat there except little packets of biscuits or sweets. And there's not much in the bakery, only some kinda buns with green icing on - didn't look too good - and some tarts filled with prunes. And the coffee – the cups were real small and they didn't have any milk."

Jay looks devastated. He recalls their honeymoon in Vienna, where each morning they'd chosen a cosy coffee house to drink hot chocolate topped with whipped cream, and eat sachertorte. Back in London the small tea shop near their home serves sticky gingerbread, lemon drizzle cake, flapjacks, and scones with cream and jam.

They are not going to find anything like that round here. In this part of very rural France the majority of the local population are retired farmers who pop into the bar/café for a little glass of red wine or a small cup of coffee and a chat. They don't buy cakes. I did once ask for a hot chocolate, which was made by mixing some hot water with some pale chocolate powder and adding a little cold milk. It wasn't very nice.

I try to cheer Jay up by telling him that not far away is an English tea room serving a wondrous variety of cakes and pastries, as well as an excellent assortment of teas, coffees and hot chocolate. Or, if they drive up to town, they'll find excellent cakes and biscuits.

But he says that won't be same as walking to the village each morning, with Thomas, to sit in a pretty café sipping hot drinks and eating cream cakes.

Reluctantly Thomas goes for a walk twice a day, hauled along on the end of his lead. Sam and Jay take it in turns to wear the black and white overcoat, which fits Jay but looks like a reefer jacket on Samantha. They do not have suitable footwear for trudging around wet fields, and have to hang their shoes to dry from a nail in the beam over the stove, which Jay is still having difficulty in lighting and keeping alight.

Their shock and disillusionment about the village takes second place to their horror when they venture out at night for the first time and discover there is no street lighting.

"Jeez - you daren't drive on these roads at night," wails Jay. "You're for sure going to end up dead in a ditch. It's so damned dark here – like being in Hell."

Darkness is a big issue, and not just on the roads. All three of them are frightened of the night. Having lived most of their lives either in Hollywood or London, they are used to bright light, and plenty of it. They have never experienced the kind of darkness you find in an isolated hamlet in the middle of French nowhere in the depths of winter. And in our hamlet, the winter nights are very, very dark.

Thomas will only go outside the door at night if Jay and Sam both go with him. Neither Sam nor Jay will go further than the gate on their own. Last night they saw "Victorian faces" peering into the bathroom window - some 15 ft. above ground level, the same Victorian faces that they have noticed hovering in the hedges. They say that Thomas is now sleeping upstairs on the bed with them, for protection. I think they mean they are protecting him. He is a sweet but extraordinarily nervous dog.

This morning the three of them are huddled on my doorstep, looking worn and grey.

"Look, honey, we're real scared. There's something crazy going on. Things moving around in the night. We can hear them."

"That's only because there's no ambient noise," I explain breezily.

"You'd hear the same noises anywhere if there wasn't traffic around. It's natural movement in the house, wind, mice...."

Samantha shrieks.

"Next door," I hastily add. "In the neighbour's barn. Nowhere near you."

"It's so dark," says Jay. "We're not used to it. It's like a horror movie."

I give them a supply of tea lights, and suggest they burn them through the night.

Next morning they are back on the doorstep with some freaky news.

"We watched those little candles all night," says Jay, "and you aren't going to believe what happened."

Had they maybe set something on fire, I wonder.

"Suddenly they went out. All of them. At EXACTLY THE SAME TIME."

Sam clings to him. "Yeah, it was so spooky. Poof, poof, poof ..... Like an evil spirit blew them out. "

"That's because they are all the same size," I explain gently. "They all burn for the same length of time. That's why they go out together."

They don't look convinced.

Next morning the trio are back with even more disturbing news.

"We didn't sleep a minute the whole night. There was some weird creepy noise coming from the roof. Like something was running about on it. Little tapping noises. Real fast. For a couple of hours. Tap tap tap tap tap tap tap ... What do you think that could have been?"

"It was rain," I say. "Raindrops." They stare at me suspiciously.

The Victorian faces continue popping up in the hedges and behind cars, and I wonder if it is anything to do with the funny cigarettes Jay and Samantha smoke. Although I am sometimes exasperated by their naïveté and timidity, I am really very fond of them, and wish that somehow I could make their stay less terrifying.

Sam is a novelty in a land where the average height of its inhabitants is 5ft 2" (1.5 metres). When she drags Thomas out for his walks, the neighbours stand at their windows to watch, and when she goes into the village she stops the traffic.

They've been here for three traumatic weeks, and come to say that they're going to Germany for Christmas to stay with a distant relative who lives beside a castle on the Rhine. I ask if they aren't worried about ghosts, in view of all the legends about hauntings in old castles.

Samantha turns to Jay and says "Is that right? Do they have ghosts there?"

"Of course not. There aren't any ghosts in Germany." But there's a note of uncertainty in his voice.

While they're away I go in every so often to light the fire and keep the damp at bay. Every inch of Pissenlit is jammed with suitcases, sacks of dog food, and huge heaps of newspapers and magazines. However have they managed to survive in this mess for so long?

When they return from Germany, Samantha and Jay bring me a belated Christmas present of a stollen cake and a large jar of goose fat. Over a coffee and cake session, I suggest that they use Lavande to store as many of their things as possible so that they have more room in Pissenlit.

"Actually, honey, we've decided to move on," says Jay. "We talked about it, and we're just too scared to stay here any longer. We're moving down to the Med for the next couple of months. No offence - we love you - but we can't spend another night here."

They pile all their belongings into their car, and come to say their farewells.

Samantha hugs me to her stomach for a long moment, patting my hair, and then Jay clutches me to his chest and rocks gently from side to side.

"Listen, honey, listen to me. I know what I'm talking about, and there's some real bad stuff going on here. Evil forces are at work. Please, please, get out while you still can. Believe me, you've gotta get away. Sam and I love you, and we don't want to be learning about your terrible death on the TV. There's still time. Sell up and go. Or just go. Leave all this behind and move somewhere nice. This is such a bad place."

He takes my face in his hands and looks into my eyes. "Promise me, babe. Listen to Uncle Jay. Go while you still can."

I am really sad to see them go. They're nuts; but I love them.

Looking back at our first year as holiday-home owners, I feel it hasn't gone too badly. Apart from Sam and Jay and the couple with the baby, all our guests have gone away happy and several have booked for next year. Although I had originally had some concerns about my privacy, I have enjoyed meeting new people and their pleasure in being here. Yes, I think it's gone pretty well.

Chapter Ten

Year Two – Barefaced Cheek and New Baby

NO. 4 (also known, I have since learned from other unhappy employers, as The Ladies' Front Bottom) turns up one April afternoon, waving a bunch of beetroots and four Tesco Value sliced white loaves.

"Present for you," he calls.

"What do you want?" I ask.

"Could you lend me €50 ($65)?"

"WHAT?"

"I've moved out from Sophie's. She's taken against Monty - kicked him last night. Didn't she, Monty?"

Monty gazes from No. 4 to me with sad eyes.

"Hitting me is one thing. But nobody touches me dog. I've nowhere to sleep, no food for Monty, and no petrol. €50 would get me through until tomorrow. I think you still owe for the work I did here."

My mouth opens and closes in speechless astonishment.

"I'm not giving you money, you still owe me for the work you didn't finish. You can sleep in Pissenlit tonight, and I'll give you food for Monty."

"Yes, but then there's me car. I need fuel."

"That's not my problem, I'm afraid."

"Well, if you could just let me have twenty ..."

"You can have a bed for tonight, food for Monty and I'll feed you. That's it. Tomorrow, you're on your own."

"Ta, missus. Appreciate that. Come on Monty, tea time." He walks into the kitchen, switches on the kettle, takes some slices from one of the loaves and pops them in the toaster. He smothers them in butter and sits munching and slurping contentedly.

"So, we don't know where we'll be tomorrow, do we, Monty?" Monty rolls his eyes and wags his feathery tail.

Always being a sucker for anyone in difficulty, I force myself not to weaken. I lend No. 4 a sleeping bag and give him some tins of dog food.

"Cheers," he says. "But if you could just let me have petrol money then I'll be out of your way tomorrow."

"You'd better be out anyway," I said. "Be gone in the morning, because there are quite a few people looking for you, and I don't want any trouble here."

That's true. No. 4 has let down everybody who has employed him in the area, and there's talk of stolen machinery too.

I hear him next morning, very early, in the kitchen, whistling and making himself breakfast. I venture downstairs when I hear his car drive away, and see that he's taken the loaves with him, but left the beetroot. I suppose there's not a lot you can do with a bunch of beetroot if you're homeless. And I can't help being impressed by his effrontery.

At the end of May a letter arrives, bearing a Belfast post mark. It contains two photographs. One shows a crumpled little baby, and written on the back: "Baby John

- Made in France," and in the second a proud, beaming James and Ellen gazing at a small bundle. Their afternoon siestas have borne fruit.

Chapter Eleven

Year Two – Lamenting Hens and Malevolent Storms

OUR first summer guests for our second year are a house-hunting couple in their late 30s, who have brought her father with them. He's a dignified, delightful man, a retired building engineer who is going to advise them on a suitable property. I've warned them it will be a tight fit in Pissenlit for three adults, but as they're going to be away all day they only want somewhere to sleep as they'll be eating out.

Alec, the father is sleeping on the futon in the living area. It's one of the items I bought from Tristram. On their fourth day, Simon and Angela find their dream property, in the neighbouring Charente departement; Alec has given it his seal of approval, and they've signed a compromis – an agreement to buy. That leaves them two days to relax before returning to England. During that time they invite me for drinks. I am horrified when I sit on the futon. It's like sitting on a concrete bench with a thin cushion on top. I am mortified to know that poor Alec has been sleeping on it for four days, but they are most gracious and Alec assures me he has been quite comfortable. When they leave, having committed themselves to tens of thousands of Pounds to buy their new home, Simon writes in the guest book: "This has been the most expensive holiday of our lives."

Lavande's first guests this year are a gentle elderly couple staying, fortunately as it will turn out for the hens, for only one week. They have come, they say, just to enjoy the quiet country life. With frogs, crickets, bats, nightingale, owls, and many other varieties of birds in our garden, I'm sure they will.

However, the morning after their arrival the old gentleman is shouting over the fence, "Miss, Miss, please come quickly."

I assume his wife must be ill, so I run round trying to remember whether I should phone the ambulance or the fire brigade first. In France, the fire brigade can often reach somebody faster than an ambulance, especially in the more isolated areas, and the firemen include members trained to deal with medical emergencies. And I must remember that to signal a heart attack in French, the terminology is "crise cardiaque" – a cardiac crisis, and not "mal au coeur" which, illogical as it might appear does not mean having a heart problem, but feeling sick. Knowing the difference could be a matter of life or death. The emergency services are unlikely to spring into action if they receive a call to say somebody is feeling bilious.

The old lady is up on her feet, next to the fence, both hands clutched against her throat. Wasp or bee sting, I think. Do I treat it with acid or alkaline? I never can remember. Bicarb or vinegar? I'm flooded with relief that she isn't collapsed on the ground.

"Are you in pain?" I ask, trying to lead her to a chair.

"Listen!" she squeals. "Listen to that poor creature."

I can't hear anything except our little group of hens chatting as they hunt in the grass for insects.

"What can you hear?" I ask.

"That terrible sound. A sort of moaning."

I can still only hear the hens.

"That noise?"

"Yes, an animal is in distress. Please find it and do something. I can't bear to listen to it."

"It's just the hens," I laugh. "That's how they talk to each other."

Blissfully unaware of the tempest they have raised in this old lady's breast, the hens continue their leisurely hunting, murmuring to each other and clucking triumphantly as they pounce on a new morsel. From the barn comes a loud squawk of satisfaction from somebody who has just laid an egg.

"Oh no! I've never heard such a noise," she continues. "It can't be right. They're in such pain."

Thank heavens we don't have sheep, cattle or even worse a donkey. As for guinea fowl – unthinkable. We rehomed our last one a few years ago because the noise it made was like sheet metal being ripped apart. What would she think if she heard them giving voice?

She really is in a tearful state and I can't convince her that the hens are just talking in their own language, so I herd them away from their favourite hunting ground right next to Lavande's garden, where they can generally be assured of fine dining – back to the far end of the field, out of earshot.

By the next morning I've forgotten all about the incident, and it is only when I take the dogs for their evening walk that the old boy calls out "Miss, Miss," again. He is sorry to complain but his wife has worried herself sick as she can hear the hens lamenting from dawn to dusk. Because she finds their noise so distressing, she has stayed indoors all day. Neither her husband nor I are able to reassure her that the rather mournful noise hens makes is quite normal, and that our hens have less reason than most to lament, as they will live out their lives in freedom, peace and comfort unlike the majority of their sisters. For the rest of their stay the girls are confined to the barn, slightly perplexed, but happy enough to scratch around in the straw.

A quiet, friendly couple from Cornwall arrive in early June. She has some fairly recent scars on her face, and is obviously sensitive about them, touching them often. Over a drink she describes a terrifying experience the previous year. While her husband was at work, and she was alone in their house, lightning struck, coming down the chimney into their living room and throwing her off the settee. It shattered the windows and set the furniture on fire, and eventually the whole house was ablaze. Her face and legs were badly cut by flying glass, and she was stunned, burned, and blinded by blood in her eyes. Neighbours had managed to get her out of the house and summoned an ambulance, and by the time her husband returned home, he found their house smouldering, surrounded by firemen, and half the roof and his wife gone.

She said that what had so unnerved her was the fact that despite the magnitude and range of the storm, theirs was the only property affected, the houses on either side escaping untouched. It made her feel as if she had somehow been the personal target of a malevolent force, a feeling that she could not shake off. She has had to have an operation on one leg to repair damage, as well as surgery to her face, and is lucky not to have lost the sight of one eye. She's still shaky when she talks about the experience. Their house has now been repaired – almost rebuilt, they said, but they have lost so many things that were special and irreplaceable, and a lingering feeling of unease means she's not certain that she wants to live there any more.

She has had to have counselling because she not only dreams frequently about the storm, but whenever she's alone finds herself sitting staring at the chimney, waiting for it to happen again. This is the first time they've been away since the event, and she wants to see how she feels when she gets back. They've lived in that house for more than twenty years, since their marriage, and brought up their children there, so have strong emotional ties to the place, and she is torn between wanting to stay and wanting to move.

Her husband confides, privately, that he is very worried about her and thinks that they will end up having to sell and move. They are both well-educated people with responsible jobs and their feet on the ground; but with her porcelain pale skin and dark red hair she's very much a Celt and definitely fey.

Rather spookily, although our weather has been perfect for several weeks, we have a crashing storm one day, with thunder and lightning, and the irrational thought occurs to me that maybe it's come here to look for her. However, she's unfazed. "It's not the lightning that worries me. It's the spirit of our house," she says. "Something has changed. It no longer feels kind."

Remembering Jay and Samantha's terror when they had stayed here and their dire warnings of evil spirits, I ask casually whether she has picked up any strange vibes in Pissenlit, and she shakes her head. "No, it feels good here. Have you had anything strange happen?"

No, I reply, it's always felt like a very benevolent place. There's nothing weird going on here.

I may have spoken too soon.

Morris and Deana, friends who also own some holiday homes a few miles from here say that they never get to know any of their guests, because apart from meeting them on arrival, they never see them again unless something goes wrong.

"They're just names on paper," says Deana. "I don't know how you can put up with having strangers so close, all through the summer. I'd hate it."

But my experience is exactly the opposite, and despite Carole's earlier concerns, I very much enjoy meeting our guests and don't find their presence at all intrusive. Being fascinated by human behaviour, I'm finding plenty to keep me entertained.

Chapter Twelve
Year Two – The Romance of Lemon Juice

RICK is one of those men who manage to be very attractive despite being overweight, carelessly dressed and badly groomed. He reminds me of Russell Crowe. Jenny is slim and blonde with grey, tired eyes. Rick does all the cooking, waits on her, and picks flowers for her. They go for long walks holding hands, and when they come back he massages her feet. Twice they have invited me to eat with them, and have served the kind of wine we only buy for special occasions. Rick is a bon viveur, and a serial husband. Stroking Jenny's hand, and blowing her frequent kisses, he explains why, as much as he loves her, he'll never marry her.

"This lady," he says, "is everything I could ever want. She's beautiful, intelligent, sexy, caring. She's my perfect woman."

Jenny smiles enigmatically.

"But," Rick tops up our glasses, "she's the fifth absolutely perfect woman in my life, and I'm not going to spoil things this time by marrying her."

"You've been married four times?"

"Yes, four mistakes. I'm a slow learner," he smiles ruefully.

"What went wrong?"

"We got married."

"And then?"

"I didn't like being married. Not their fault. I still love them and we've all remained friends."

"So what was the problem?"

"Dunno really. It's a mental thing. I think it's because I'm such a romantic; I love wooing, spoiling my ladies. I need to be totally in love all the time. As soon as real life gets in the way ... something goes wrong." Rick shakes his head sadly. Jenny keeps calmly sipping her wine.

"All my ladies have been blondes, like Jenny. And they're all gentle souls, really lovely people. If you put them in a line, you'd say they were sisters."

Jenny laughs. "It's true. He's got all these photographs all over his house, of women who look like me. I call us the Stepford Wives."

Rick opens a second bottle of chilled Chablis Grand Cru, and wraps his arms around her as he refills her glass, resting his chin on her head and smiling at me. "True love," he whispers. My glass is served with a peck on the cheek, and an "Ummm."

They generously insist on taking me to a local restaurant for a meal on the eve of their departure. Rick is attentive, amusing and a great raconteur. In his youth he was a merchant seaman and keeps us laughing with tales of his adventures upon the waves and below decks. He's also been a radio presenter which, he says, was a particularly chaotic episode in his life, and had owned his own greengrocery which had been a great success until a major supermarket built a local branch and took all his customers.

"Yes," he muses, "everything always went so well, until it all went wrong. But, still, I've enjoyed every minute of my life."

An exquisitely tangy tarte au citron for dessert stirs a memory for Rick. "There are many uses for lemons, as you may know, but here's one you may not have heard of. I am going to divulge the secret of the little bottle of lemon juice, something passed to me by my Greek friend, Yanni, when I was in the merchant marine."

"You see," he explains, "it's fine to have a girl in every port – even better to have several girls in every port – but a fellow has to be careful. Girls in ports can give a man who doesn't want to wear wellies in the bath more than just a good time."

Jenny and I giggle dutifully.

"An unwanted souvenir, if you understand what I mean."

We nod our understanding.

"So, Yanni explains to me that he has a fail-safe method of ensuring that you take nothing away except a happy memory. You always carry a small bottle of lemon juice in your pocket, in case it's your lucky day. If you strike gold, so to speak, at the appropriate moment you unscrew the little bottle and pour some juice into your hand. Then, skilfully, you apply it to the lady's garden gateway."

Jenny has to hold her laugh in with her hands. Her eyes are streaming, her shoulders heaving.

"You mean," she gasps, "you splash lemon juice all over her privates?"

83

"Precisely! If the lady doesn't react, then you know that you're safe to proceed. But if she yelps, or squeals, or jumps up and down, then you know it's time for a short sharp exit."

I try to imagine how I would react under the circumstances, and decide that if anybody splashed lemon juice in my garden gateway I'd punch them in the face and kick them in the balls.

It's a good story, and we all end up weeping with laughter. Rick excuses himself to visit the gents, and while he's away, Jenny says: "He is such a sweetie, a really lovely guy. I'm terribly fond of him. But the fact is that it's his wives who have left him. He's completely irresponsible. He tries so hard, but gets himself into such dreadful messes and can never pay the bills. And he never learns. Eventually, they can't take any more. It's like being married to an adorable but uncontrollable child. I met him a couple of months after Number Four left – as a matter of fact I knew her from art classes, she's a charming woman. He was devastated when she went. At the moment he thinks he's in love with me, because he always has to be in love with somebody. He's great company, but I'm not in love with him. I suppose what I feel for him is mostly maternal."

Rick returns and gives her a hug and kiss. "Oooh," he says, "you are such a beautiful woman. Je t'adore."

They're leaving at 6.00 am next day, so we say our farewells after dinner. Back home, Rick sees me to my door, and gives me a hug, a peck on each cheek, and then, quite unexpectedly kisses me passionately and murmurs that next year he'll come back alone. It wouldn't surprise me at all. As he says, he really is an incurable romantic.

Chapter Thirteen
Year Two – Mrs Mop to the Rescue

I'VE realised what a twit I was to make such a fuss over the cleaning. I picked up a tip from the web – wear a gardening apron to carry around all the necessary products and cloths, and a bag to put rubbish in. It's so simple, really, and now I have the hang of it, it no longer worries me. A couple of hours each week is all it takes.

A new family arrives in a people-carrier, with four children and six bicycles. They're here for a fortnight. The eldest girl is 14 and the youngest 5. The parents seem frightfully jolly, and delighted with Lavande.

"Marvellous," chortles father, "right at the end here, with no traffic. It'll be great for the kids. We won't have to worry about them playing out."

"No, they'll be perfectly safe," I assure them.

"Oh good!" says the mother, "We can get away from the little sods and enjoy ourselves. Talk about ready for a holiday!"

As soon as they've unloaded their baggage and bicycles, the parents come to ask where the nearest bar is. I give them directions down to the village, and the mother shoves her husband playfully in the back towards their car, saying "Lead on MacDuff, take me to the vino," and away they drive.

Half an hour later I see the children standing in a quiet huddle at the back door of the cottage. They are pale, spotty, withdrawn and seem rather sullen, so I ask if they would like to come with me and meet the dogs and horses.

"No," says the eldest girl. The other children move closer to her. "We don't like animals."

Perhaps they'd like to play boules, I suggest, and show them where they can play, and explain how the game works, but they are listless and unresponsive and wander back into the cottage, leaving me feeling ineffectual and uncomfortable.

The family's daily routine is unvaried. They surface late morning and the parents drive off to the bar, returning in the early evening for a couple of hours before going back to the bar again. The children never come out and resist all my attempts to befriend them. I feel a strong sense of injustice for this little band, left to amuse themselves every day, something they don't seem to be able to do. No, they would not like me to show them where they can ride their bicycles. They accept a bowl of raspberries, but don't want any lettuce or eggs, thank you. When I ask what they eat, the eldest girl says that she makes chips and burgers for them all for lunch. I am aghast at the thought of her with a hot chip pan, but she tells me that they have brought a deep-fat fryer with them and she is used to cooking with it.

The parents don't seem to find anything unusual about leaving them to fend for and entertain themselves, all day, in a strange house in a foreign country. They are unabashedly enjoying themselves at the bar – which as a matter of fact is quite a dreary place – and admit they're glad to get away from their children. I give them a fistful of brochures showing various activities and outings for families, and recommend the local park and lake as a good place for swimming. Or they can hire canoes, or visit the monkey park.

"Nah," says Mum, "they don't like going out. They're happier on their own. They never go out. Don't worry about them, they entertain themselves."

It isn't my business. It's their holiday, and their children are not my responsibility. But it does worry me.

There are two ladies staying in Pissenlit, a professional harpist and her cousin. The harpist has brought with her a tuning bowl, which she plays for several hours each day to keep in practice for her harping. It is a most exquisite instrument, a smooth wooden bowl with strings stretched across it, which give off beautiful musical notes when plucked. She lets me have a go, and despite having the musical talent of a feather duster, I produce some haunting sounds. I decide that I'll buy one of the bowls for myself. How much would one expect to pay, I ask. "This one," she says, cost "£1,900 ($3,000)." Perhaps I won't buy one after all.

They mention the family in Lavande, and remark that it's quite odd for parents not to spend any time with their children, but they feel it is best not to interfere, and leave them to get on with it.

We have a video machine that we no longer use, so I take it round to ask if the children would like to borrow it. For the first time they show signs of animation, and ask what films we have on tape. What kind of films do they enjoy, I ask. The oldest girl shrugs and says "anything", and one of the two boys, who is about seven, jumps up and down and yells "Chucky, Chucky, Chucky!" while his older brother mumbles something about the Texas Chainsaw Massacre. The children assure me they know how to connect up the video to the television. So I leave them to it, with a box of tapes which they rummage through and start squabbling over, although the boys are going to be disappointed because none of the tapes are bloodthirsty horror films.

When they've been here a week, as the parents prepare for another trip "down the bar," I ask, "Don't the children ever want to go out?"

They stare at me as if I am a simpleton babbling in a foreign tongue.

"There are plenty of places round here that they would enjoy. It's a shame for them not to get out a bit, don't you think?"

They gaze in genuine, silent bafflement, then the mother says, "Nah, they're happier as they are. They'd of rather stayed at home than come with us. Pity they aren't older so we could of left them behind."

However, I think our brief conversation may have had some slight impact, or maybe the expression on my face conveyed my feelings and pricked their conscience, because when they came home from the bar yesterday evening, they bundled the kids into the car and vanished for a couple of hours, waving and giving a thumbs up. I was watering the plants when they came back, and they yelled that they'd all had a great time at the bar. The kids loved it!

Poor little devils.

This morning, to my surprise, I see them all mounting their bicycles.

"We're off," calls out the father.

"Have a good time," I say. "Are you going somewhere exciting?"

"Yes, we're going to Villeville. We've heard there's a great bar there, by the river."

Villeville is almost twenty miles away by the shortest route, which is a busy main road and there are two or three very steep hills. It's already a scorching day. The kids look miserable. None of them are wearing helmets or hats.

"Take plenty of water with you. It's a long way, especially in this heat."

He laughs and waves his hand dismissively. "We'll stop and get some on the way if we need to." Away they pedal.

I'm pleased the children are finally going out, but worried that they are undertaking a long journey on such a hot day.

It's just after 5.00 pm when the father arrives back, alone. He is staggering, and crimson in the face. They didn't get to Villeville, he says. They're hungry and knackered. The supermarket was closed for lunch and they couldn't buy any water. He's left the children sitting on the roadside in tears, completely exhausted. His wife is furious that they've wasted a day, and there's no way for them to get home apart from cycling, which they are too tired to do. So he has cycled back - it's taken him nearly three hours - and must now take the car to go to collect them.

When they finally reach home they slink into the cottage and the lights all go off immediately.

Next day their white faces are all burnt red, and they have reverted to the original agenda: parents off to the bar, kids left here to manage on their own. I take them a bottle of lotion to soothe their sunburn, and they glare at me reproachfully. I will never interfere again. I can't wait for them to leave.

When they do, the children go silently, sitting pinch-faced in the people-carrier, the bicycles strapped to the vehicle. The parents have been to the bar for a last session, leaving the kids to clean the cottage. It is, the parents say, their best ever holiday. They have filled four pages of the guest book with rapturous eulogies to the bar. They have had a wonderful time, and promise they will be back next year.

With new-found confidence in my cleaning skills, and armed with the gardening apron, bucket and mop, I go to prepare the cottage for the next arrivals. I skid across the tiled kitchen floor and bang my elbow on the work surface as I go down. The walls, units and sink are smothered in grease, and the floor is like a skating-rink. There are two live caterpillars underneath the microwave, and the sink is blocked with something grey and lumpy. All the crockery and cutlery is pushed out of sight, unwashed. There are sodden towels lying on the filthy beds. I can hardly bear to clean the loo. In every room there are heaps of sweet papers, fluff and dirty tissues pushed into the corners.

In less than four hours the next guests will arrive, and it is 36ºC (97°F) in the shade. By the time I have made the place habitable – I use lots of bleach - I am dizzy, exhausted and angry. I am never going to deal with such a horrible mess again.

I put up some cards in the local supermarkets, and spread the word to friends that I need a cleaning person. It's very difficult to find anybody; we live several miles from the nearest town; most of the local population are either retired farmers advanced in years whose wives have earned their rest, or English immigrants with sufficient money not to need to work. After a fortnight I have almost given up hope when somebody tells me of an Englishwoman who may be available.

"She needs the money because her husband did a moonlight flit. Can't blame him, poor man, the way she treated him. But she may be more trouble than she's worth. She's very strange."

As long as she can wield a mop, drive a vacuum-cleaner, clean bathrooms and kitchens and make beds, she can be as strange as she likes. I'm not planning to establish any kind of relationship with her other than employer/employee. I phone her number and have a rambling and surreal conversation which includes the difficulties she is having with her French neighbours, who hate her, and something about a problem with the handle of her cooker, but I think she has agreed to come and discuss the cleaning role. I have asked her to come next Saturday morning at 10.30am, when the guests will have left the cottages. I'm not totally convinced she has understood.

On Wednesday afternoon a tall thin woman of a certain age is standing at the gate looking rather confused, dressed in a flowery blue-patterned frock with a frilly peplum, staggeringly high heels and a blue turban with a feather on the front held in place by a large brooch. Her face is thickly coated in pancake make-up. She looks as if she is on her way to a fancy dress party.

"Anybody there?" she calls.

"Hello, are you lost?" I ask.

"Not if you're the grande dame looking for a domestic engineer," she replies. "I'm Ivy Pinson. You asked me to come today."

"Oh. The cleaning lady. You're meant to come on Saturday morning, don't you remember? I can't show you round the cottages now, there are people staying in them."

She says that she must have misunderstood me, but her tone implies that the fault is mine. As she's standing expectantly at the gate, and has taken such care with her appearance to come to talk about a cleaning job, I invite her in for a cup of tea.

"I'd prefer a cold drink, if you wouldn't mind terribly," she says, fanning her face with a magazine she has picked up from the table.

"It's dreadfully hot. Do you have any wine?"

While I'm digging a bottle of rosé out of the fridge, she's opened a cabinet and taken out one of our best and largest crystal goblets.

"Hm, Waterford. I love nice things, don't you?"

She pings it with her forefinger, filling the air with the hiss of fading bells. I bring her a glass of wine in a plain glass and deftly remove the Waterford back to the cabinet. It's the last of a set of six.

Taking off her turban gingerly, she shakes her head and ruffles her thick blonde hair. As she swigs the wine in large gulps, she chirrups away about a great many people I have never heard of. They all have one thing in common: horrible things have happened to them. She nudges her glass towards me with a raised eyebrow. I refill it half-way: she has to drive home. While she talks, her eyes are constantly flicking around the room as if she is taking an inventory. The bright afternoon light picks up a network of deep lines beneath the thick make-up, and the artfully knotted scarf around her neck does not completely hide folds of loose skin. I estimate that she is in her mid-seventies, and am intrigued as to why she is looking for a cleaning job.

Interrupting her in mid-sentence as she describes a young woman who committed suicide by standing in front of a train, I steer the conversation around to the purpose of her being here, which is to clean the cottages before each new arrival. Is that really the sort of thing she wants to do?

In a lowered voice she tells me that "since that cowardly little shit ran off" she is living hand to mouth, with no income except from the miserable interest on a very small nest-egg that is being rapidly depleted by the increasing cost of living in France. She is desperate and ready to do anything, anything at all, to keep body and soul together.

I make one of my classic gaffes, putting my pied firmly into my bouche.

"But surely you get the British State pension?" I say.

She slams her glass onto the table, making me jump. (Thank heaven I had the foresight to remove the Waterford earlier.)

"Me? Pension? Of course not. Not for years. How ever could you suggest such a thing?"

As I kick myself vigorously on the ankle, she rearranges her face and smiles brightly.

"No, fortunately it will still be many years before I become a senior citizen."

She tilts her empty glass from side to side suggestively.

"No, what I was going to say was that you have it to look forward to," I say, lamely, picking up the glass. "Although, of course, I realise not for a long time yet. Dear me. You don't know whether to look forward to it or not!"

As a distraction I jump up and make a pot of hibiscus tea, then we get down to business.

"I'll pay you €15 ($20) for each clean/change-over you do. Some weeks it'll be both cottages, and other weeks just one, depending on how long people stay. But we are fully booked until the end of September, so it should keep you busy for quite a few weeks."

"€15 to clean two cottages? Oh no. That sounds like exploitation."

"No, €15 for each cottage; some weeks one, some weeks two. That's what I meant."

She pushes away her tea cup.

"Forgive me, it tastes like cats' piss. You should explain yourself more clearly," she admonishes.

"And mileage," she continues. "It's quite a long way for me to come. I'll need something towards travelling costs."

Although I hadn't bargained for that, if she only knew, she could charge just about anything, so desperate am I not to have the weekly threat of cleaning hanging over my head. It will reduce our profit, but next year I'll build it into the rent. I agree a further €2 ($2.50) per visit.

While she is using the downstairs bathroom the phone rings. From the living room I hear her heels clacking about upstairs as I'm answering the call, but when I go back into the hall she is sitting at the table flicking through my post. I steer her out to her car, and will look forward to seeing her at 11.00 am on Saturday, when both sets of guests will be leaving and she can anticipate a profitable day.

"See you tomorrow," she calls, waggling her fingers from the car window, and clipping the gate pillar as she reverses her car.

"No!" I yell as she disappears down the lane, "Saturday!"

Remembering the warning that she would probably drive me mad, I note that already I am screaming.

In the distance brakes squeal, and a couple of minutes later, friends arrive unexpectedly.

"Nearly had the car written off down the lane," says Mike. "Bloody woman was all over the road. Surely she hasn't been here?"

"She's my Mrs. Mop, going to clean the cottages for me. She's absolutely hilarious!"

Sheila pulled a face. "She's many things, but hilarious isn't one of them. That's why her name fits her so well: Ivy Pinson, otherwise known as Poison Ivy."

"I found her amusing. She is obviously batty, but she can't be that awful."

Sheila looks at me over the top of her spectacles in a meaningful way. "I hope you're right," she says.

Chapter Fourteen

Year Two – Micky Poo-Poo And My Cowboy Friend

LAVANDE'S new guests had phoned to ask if there is a safety gate for the stairs, as they have a 4-year-old who "is everywhere at once."

I remember we do have one, left over from years ago when we had a litter of puppies, to stop them from climbing stairs when they were very young – it puts too much strain on their joints. I dig it out from the barn.

Four-year-old Micky is an enchanting little boy with large brown eyes and cheruby lips in a permanent smile. While the family are unpacking after a long drive on a hot day, Micky has wriggled out of his car seat and set off at a determined trot into the next door garden, shouting "I'm here, I'm here, Granny!"

Mrs Nextdoor, who has been pulling up dandelions to feed to her rabbits, is surprised but delighted to meet this small stranger who runs up to her, takes her hand and tugs her towards various cages housing future meals for her family.

"What's this, chicken?" he asks. "What's this? Rabbit?"

In that mysterious way that old and young span the communication chasm, she shows him around her garden, pointing out the various creatures living behind bars, while he chatters on excitedly until his father calls to him.

"Bye, Granny," he says, and walks in an important way back to his father, calling that Granny has shown him all her pets.

"He's a very sociable little fellow," says Jack, "but we have to keep an eye on him every minute. He moves like greased lightning."

Jack and Belinda are first-time parents in their mid-forties, and little Micky is clearly the centre of their world. Every moment of their day revolves around him. They've brought a paddling pool, and most of the day I can hear Micky laughing and singing and splashing about in the water, and the adults shrieking as he tips water over them, or running after him as he tries to climb over the fence, or up a tree, or over the gate. Jack's sister Eileen takes turns at entertaining Micky so that his mother and father have an hour or so to rest once in a while.

There isn't a daylight moment when Micky can't be heard asking questions, singing, laughing, shouting and very, very occasionally, screaming. I imagine that's when he's tired. And after the first three days I'm beginning to feel like screaming too, sometimes, because as adorable as he is, Micky is wearing me out, and I'm not even one of the family.

I'm used to sound coming from our guests; I'd be alarmed if it wasn't. Most people are considerate and play their music at a reasonable volume; the only time that the decibels tend to peak is late at night after a few bottles. It's "random sound," in that it varies in pitch, duration and tone, unlike Micky-sound which is repetitive and constant. In the rare moments Micky isn't making a noise, one of the family is calling him, or singing for him, or teaching him nursery rhymes, and my head is filled with Micky. Even the cats, who usually spend the day with our guests in the hope of picking up extra food, are keeping clear of Lavande. I begin to yearn for nightfall, when Micky will be tucked up in his cot and quiet for a few blissful hours.

I love little Micky, he's a gorgeous little boy and a delight to see and hear; he's bright, happy, well-behaved, and what more could you ask of a 4-year-old? He's probably perfect. Just not for a whole week. He seems to have almost supernatural stamina and energy, which I admire and envy.

"I don't know where Micky gets all his oomph from," laughs Belinda, as we pass on the lane. Looking at their happy, haggard faces, I think he's draining it directly from them.

While they're here, Micky develops a new talent.

"Sooosssssssssie," he calls through the fence. "I did a big long poo-poo!"

"Well done, Micky," I say.

The following day he announces proudly that he did lots of little round poos. Belinda is concerned, and buys Bran Flakes.

Before they leave, Micky has accomplished a squishy and two more longs. I wonder if it's quite normal for a child to take such an interest in its faecal achievements? I don't remember my children doing so, but I don't want to spoil Micky's fun, so I congratulate him on every update, and when they leave at the end of the week, and Micky is strapped into the car, singing, I wave farewell, and then, idiotically, I call out "Happy poo-poos, Micky."

After they've gone I make a quick check to make sure that there won't be any nasty shocks for Ivy – I don't want to lose her before she's even begun. There is an unopened packet of cereal and a packet of sugar in Lavande, a half-bottle of white wine in the fridge in Pissenlit as well as the ubiquitous jam and pepper.

Ivy arrives for her first cleaning session wearing a black 1920s-style flapper dress decorated with jet beads, a matching beaded headband with a small feather arising from it, and a jet bead choker. I'm concerned that she's going to have difficulty getting the vacuum cleaner up the stairs in stiletto heels, and start to wonder whether she's the right choice for our cleaner. Then I remember she's our only choice.

I show her where the cleaning products and clean linen are kept, and explain how I want her to do things, then leave her to get on with it while I pick some flowers and organise the welcome packs.

She's finished in an hour, and is "utterly parched and dangerously dehydrated." No, she doesn't want a cup of tea, it's far too hot. She'll have a glass of wine. While she does so she chatters away about her awful neighbours and the beastliness of the French in general. For the first time I notice that she talks in a slightly irritating and affected nasal drawl. I make sympathetic murmurs and try to change the subject, but she isn't going to be deflected. Having slaughtered the neighbours, the French, somebody who overtook her on her way here and the bank who have just lowered the interest rate on deposit accounts, she puts on a bright smile, and says: "You are such a good listener. It's been a great help to talk to you. A problem shared is, as they say, a problem halved."

I nod sagely.

When I see her to her car I notice that on the front passenger seat is half a bottle of white wine, a packet of sugar and an unopened cereal packet.

Brad has been my penpal for several years. He lives in Oklahoma and has two obsessions, or maybe manias would be more apt. They are French history and French food. He writes that he spends all day, every day, cooking in his custom-built kitchen which cost him more than most people pay for a whole house. With self-cleaning windows and automatic blinds, a walk-in refrigerator/freezer, professional range, chiller, slicer, various food processors, the finest Japanese knives and a pasta machine, Brad's kitchen is equipped to a level that Marco Pierre White would envy.

Every year he comes to France to visit top restaurants, historic places and châteaux, and he's spent several holidays at cookery schools in Lyon. Currently he is cooking his way through Escoffier, with the intention of trying every recipe, of which he tells me there are almost 5,000. However, he will avoid any that involve eating offal of any kind, or raw fish. After cooking many of the meat dishes he only tastes a mouthful, giving the rest away to his neighbours for their dogs because he doesn't eat pork, mutton or chicken himself, only beef, and turkey at Thanksgiving. I imagine how delighted the dogs must be when they see Brad coming.

When I ask why he cooks things he has no intention of eating, or desire to eat, he replies that his passion is for cooking, not necessarily for eating, although he is very particular about what he eats. Some days he cooks, say, a chicken dish that goes to the dogs, and a beef dish for his own meal. Most days he sends me a detailed description of what he has cooked, even though I have mentioned several times that I am a pescatarian and quite squeamish about descriptions of skinning, boning, jointing, and trimming off fat. I think this message goes unread, but I enjoy our correspondence because of his enthusiasm.

Brad relishes an opportunity to use his gadgets, and scours the Internet to find gizmos he does not have, to add them to his collection. He has one that can smell whether or not meat is fresh, just in case his nose lets him down. He writes beautiful descriptions of the latest ingredients he has sourced, like reindeer milk cheese, or Maui onions that are so sweet you can eat them like apples. His latest craze is sugar work. He has mastered spirals and cages, which he crushes up and throws away once he has perfected them.

In those rare brief moments when he is not cooking, Brad reads about or watches films about French history. He's quite an authority on the subject and seems to know about every event of note since the birth of Clovis. That is the sum total of what I know about Brad.

He is planning his annual trip to France, staying in luxury hotels and châteaux, and eating at Michelin-starred restaurants. Could he spend a few days here, he asks. He mentions that he is allergic to fresh paint, feather pillows, and cats. It's going to be slightly awkward keeping the cats away, but as we have a few days vacant in Pissenlit, I can put him in there. He asks what the name Pissenlit signifies, and I tell him quite truthfully that it's the French word for a dandelion. Some innate sense tells me not to expand on the subject.

Long ago there was a film called "The Oklahoman," and I seem to remember the title character was a long, lean, weather-beaten cowboy. That is the image I have of Brad, which sits strangely with the cooking/historian.

He is coming by train from Paris to spend four days here. Then he'll hire a car to drive back to Paris and continue his tour. I'll meet him at the station, and should have no difficulty in recognising him. Lanky, suntanned cowboys are a rarity around here. But just to be safe, I ask him for a description.

He emails, saying: "I'm 5'4", not much hair, and I'll be carrying a child's backpack." I smile to myself. I like people with a sense of humour.

I spot him immediately when he jumps down onto the platform from the train. He's a bit over 6', wearing tight-fitting jeans, cowboy boots, a big-buckled belt, check shirt, with long grey hair tied back in a pony tail. I wave wildly and trot towards him.

"Brad!" I yell.

"Madame?" says the cowboy, politely perplexed. Behind him I spot a small solitary figure, looking nervously around the platform. He's fractionally taller than me, with a little tuft of white hair over each ear, and over his shoulder is a child's satchel with a Mickey Mouse motif.

Mumbling something unintelligible to the cowboy, I shout "Hello, Brad!"

The little man's expression is a mixture of relief, surprise and disappointment.

"I thought you'd look more French," he confesses as I shake his hand. "You know, with a nice skirt and high heels."

Hey, pardner, you're not exactly film star material.

Looking down at my shorts and sandals, I lie. "Well, I usually dress in the evening, once I've finished with the animals."

He's not impressed with the environs of the railway station. It isn't the most attractive place – railway stations often aren't – but it's not that bad, and I suggest a cup of coffee in a genuine French café. That cheers him up. He likes the little biscuit that comes with the coffee, but is slightly disappointed that nobody is wearing a beret. So far, nothing is quite as French as he has hoped, although why he should expect this area to be any different from all other parts of France he has visited, and where as far as I know berets are not currently de rigueur, I have no idea. The only place I have ever seen berets worn en masse was in the Pyrenees.

As we drive home his nose is pinned to the car window, scrutinising every blade of grass, every old stone, longing to see something historic and interesting. We make a detour to visit the battlefield where Edward the Black Prince defeated Jean le Bon at the battle of Poitiers in 1356. It is just a field with a lot of tussocks and bumpy bits, and a board showing the deployment of the English and French troops and the course of the battle. Brad is thrilled to be standing on the site of such a momentous event. He might even be on the very place where Edward or Jean had actually stood, he thinks. Then we spend an hour at the fortified abbey of Nouaillé Maupertuis, where he makes copious notes, and later we pass the remnants of the nearby castle where the defeated French king was briefly imprisoned, and that excites Brad to a very satisfying degree. He bounces up and down on the car seat like a child. But when we pull up outside chez nous, he seems to deflate.

"You live here?" he says. "Looks like you still have a lot of work to do," he adds, somewhat unnecessarily. "This isn't what I expected."

I am beginning to feel rather a fraud, as if I have dragged him across the Atlantic to all these disappointments. The scorched wilderness of the garden is not the immaculate lawn he had visualised, and we have no turrets, moats or a sweeping drive. Just the courtyard covered in the ankle-deep noisy little stones.

He's quite taken with Pissenlit, and can pass beneath the beams without smashing his head in. He tests the upstairs floorboards gingerly, asking whether it's OK for them to spring up and down. I assure him the building is safe. He closes the windows in case bugs come in.

When I've fed and organised the animals, I dress in my most French-looking skirt and a pair of heels, and prepare drinks. Despite being a self-proclaimed wine connoisseur who always orders the most expensive bottle from every menu, he finds my inexpensive offering very palatable. Shyly he produces a small packet containing a pair of delicate earrings. The centre is an oval of turquoise, from which are suspended two tiny silver leaves. He tells me this is genuine native American jewellery and that he spent a long time choosing it. He sincerely hopes that I won't be offended, or think him too forward or read anything into the gift other than a small token of our long friendship and mutual enjoyment of cooking and France. I feel very warm and protective towards this strange little man with his forthright manner. He's a one-off.

After we have savoured and discussed the merits of the wine, I serve the first course. Without the benefit of his collection of cooking equipment, nor his apparently limitless wealth, I have made quite an effort to prepare a

104

very French meal for him. We start with a French onion soup. Unfortunately his digestion cannot manage onions (except the Maui onions). However he eats the cheese and croutons and drinks the liquid and leaves the onion bits in the bowl. The smoked salmon quiche is a little too rich for his liver, and he declines the salad as his doctor has warned him to avoid raw fruit or vegetables when travelling abroad because of possible bacteria. I know he will be bowled over by the chocolate mousse, as indeed he is, tasting it delicately and pronouncing it as good as any he has ever eaten. He asks how I made it and listens raptly to the melting butter and chocolate part and the freshly squeezed orange, until I come to the eggs. He puts down his spoon in a panic.

"You mean it has raw eggs in? Don't you know that's very dangerous? You can get all kinds of terrible diseases. I can't eat that."

Our first meal isn't a startling success, but we fill him up with cheese and crackers, about which he has no qualms. At 10.00 pm sharp he takes his leave, thanks me for an excellent meal (which is very kind of him as he could hardly eat any of it), and says he'll see me at 8.00am for breakfast and hopes we can be on our way sight-seeing by 9.00am.

Thanks to the growing half-pots of jam left behind by guests, I'm able to offer him a wide selection to enjoy with his breakfast croissants and coffee before we set off on a whistle-stop tour of local attractions. First on our hit list is the remains of the nearby 11th century abbey of Saint Sauveur. Once an important place of Christian pilgrimage, successive wars and the Revolution have left only one great hexagonal tower, standing rather sadly next to a café/bar. We look at it for ten seconds, and then drive on to the martyred village of Oradour sur Glane, site of one historic event of which Brad knows nothing.

On a peaceful, sunny day in June 1944 a German Panzer division massacred 642 men, women and children of the village. They burned the bodies and threw them down a well, then destroyed the village by shelling and setting fire to it. Oradour has been preserved as a memorial to the event, just as it was found on the day following the massacre. It is an awesome testament to the horrors of war and man's inhumanity to his fellows. Hotels, offices, hairdressers, haberdashers, cafés, garages, the doctor's surgery, shops, schools and the railway station all reduced to charred ruins, collapsed timbers and bullet-scarred stones. Rusted old cars and bicycle frames fester in roofless garages; sewing machines and cast-iron pans protrude from smashed walls. There is no one adjective that can adequately sum up the barbarity that took place at Oradour sur Glane.

We walk around for half an hour. I show Brad the well where the burned bodies were thrown after the massacre, the sad list of names and ages of victims engraved in the walls – babies so young they hadn't been named, old people in their nineties - the church where the women and children were machine gunned. But Brad isn't really with me. He keeps looking anxiously at his watch and trying to walk to the exit. I think he must be so uncomfortable in this silent place of skeletal buildings and terrible memories that he needs to escape. When I ask if he has seen enough he nods, saying it's time we went for lunch, and let's go and find a restaurant.

"What did you think about Oradour?" I ask.

"It's a real shame that they've let it get that way," he replies.

"How do you mean?"

"Well, it's all coming down, isn't it? You'd think they'd clear up all that junk and stuff and rebuild it."

That's when I realise that the significance of the place has entirely passed him by.

The only restaurant that we can find on our route is rather expensive, but for want of an alternative we take a table and Brad asks whether we can have an aperitif. I order two glasses of Pineau de Charente, which he enjoys, particularly as it is something he has not heard of, so it has novelty value as well as a pleasing taste. He writes it down in a small notebook.

We opt for a set menu, and when it comes to the main course as he doesn't eat lamb, pork or chicken, nor carp which he says is a dirty fish and not fit for eating, that leaves him a choice of bavette (a French cut of beef), which he finds tough. Luckily there is an excellent cheese board in which he invests heavily, as the dessert is either fresh fruit salad or chocolate mousse, both of which are on the danger list.

All the time we are eating he fidgets on his chair and with his food, drums his fingers anxiously on the table, and keeps looking at his watch. He declines coffee because he wants to "get on quickly to see Richard." As he makes no move to pay the bill, I signal the waiter and thrust my debit card at him, crossing my fingers beneath the table. Brad thanks me for the meal, although he says that he's pretty disappointed with the local cuisine.

By now I am used to his outspoken manner, and understand that he has no intention of being rude – in fact I don't think he has any idea that by some people's standards he is doing so. He's just honest, and says what he means, so at least I know where I stand. Certainly he has some odd little ways, but I find myself feeling rather maternal towards him, as if he were a lost child. I have not managed to discover how he accumulated his wealth. He tells me his father was an engineer who had worked for some years during the 1950s drilling for oil in the Paris basin, which is where Brad acquired his passion for all things French. But his own career is veiled in mystery apart from occasional mentions of a stock portfolio.

Our next stop is somewhere that really excites Brad – the fortified château of Châlus-Chabrol, 25 miles south of Oradour. It's where Richard the Lionheart met his death. As we pull into the car park, Brad bounces up and down and claps his hands. He has wanted to visit this place for many years.

The original château and donjon date from the 11th century. There's a 17th century extension cobbled onto the older part, housing a museum of very nasty and vicious ancient weaponry, which we glance at briefly. Then we trot down the great stone steps to the 11th century kitchen with its nine foot thick walls. We find a small salamander in a damp corner, and Brad warns me not to touch it in case it has a poisonous bite.

A short distance from the château is the donjon, a circular tower where the château's inhabitants could flee to safety when under attack. The only entrance is about twenty feet above ground, and was accessed via demountable wooden ladders that were hauled up once everybody was safely inside. Stocked underground with food, water and weapons, the tower was regarded as impregnable and able to withstand siege for many weeks.

In 1199, during a contretemps with one of his vassals whom he believed had something that rightfully belonged to him, Richard the Lionheart attacked the château. In order to breach the supposedly impregnable tower, he planned to mine beneath it. Whilst he was inspecting the site, a sentry fired an arrow from the top of the tower. Unluckily for both the archer and the king, the arrow found its way through a gap in the royal armour into the royal shoulder. Infection set in. In the great hall of the château the king died of gangrene, lying in the arms of his mother, Eleanor of Aquitaine. Before he died, Richard pardoned the archer and instructed that he should not be punished. However, after his death the unfortunate man was flayed alive and torn to pieces by horses. In accordance with Richard's wishes his heart was buried in Normandy in Rouen Cathedral; his entrails were buried at Châlus, and the rest of him at the Royal Abbey of Fontevraud.

Panting with excitement, Brad rushes up the stairs to have a peek in the tower, then we canter back to the château to see the room where Richard expired. We throw a quick glance at the medieval garden where medicinal herbs grew, minstrels wrote and sang and knights and their ladies strolled in days of yore, and very soon we are back in the car. The site of one of the most dramatic events in medieval European history, the death of one of the greatest kings, the place he has wanted to visit for two decades, has held his attention for nearly 30 minutes. I have wondered why Brad doesn't carry a camera, and I think it must be because he never stands in one place long enough to use it.

"Where is that place where the other bits of Richard are buried?" he asks. "I've been to Rouen and seen where they put his heart, but I know there were some bits of him in another place."

"Fontevraud Abbey. It's where nearly all the Plantagenet dynasty are buried."

"Is Eleanor there? Can we go?"

"Yes, we can go tomorrow. It's too far for today. And you wanted to see Chenonceau tomorrow. If we leave early enough in the morning, we can see both."

"Let's do that!" Brad boings up and down on the seat again. "And may I take you out to eat tonight? Somewhere we can get some decent food?"

On the way home he yells from time to time whenever we pass an ancient church, an old well, or any building with turrets or tall gates. "Oh gee - look at that big old château!" he cries, pointing to a distant grain silo.

We have a modest and unremarkable meal at a local restaurant, and Brad is anxious when I order catfish, saying that it is a dirty kind of fish that eats dirty things. Then we have an early night, because tomorrow is going to be a busy day. I am up just after 6.00am to see to all the animals. The guests in Lavande have kindly agreed to keep an eye on the dogs until we get back. By 8.30am we are on our way to Fontevraud Abbey, 100 miles away. It's a vast and splendid building with a fascinating history, but Brad is only interested in looking at the tombs and effigies of Richard and Eleanor. We're out of there in half an hour and heading towards Chenonceau, 60 miles (100 miles) away. Brad, I have realised, is the historical equivalent of a train spotter. He isn't bothered about riding on the footplate, he just wants to be able to tick off the numbers.

The day is still young, so I mention that if he is interested we will be passing very close to the château at Ussé, the epitome of a romantic French château, a mixture

110

of Gothic and Renaissance architecture set amongst formal gardens and claiming to have inspired the story of the Sleeping Beauty.

As well as the splendours of the château itself, one narrow circular wing houses an exhibition of wax figures depicting the fairy tale. As we wind our way up the stone staircase we stop to peer through a small window at the baby Beauty in her cradle; a few more steps, another window - the evil witch pricking the baby's finger; and at the top of the staircase the handsome prince awakening the princess with a kiss.

Maybe he's a little tired after hiking up the steps, because Brad slows down as we take a tour around the gardens. For the first time he is doing more than merely adding a name to the list of places he has visited; he's actually looking at details and commenting on them instead of constantly studying his watch.

It's an hour's drive to Chenonceau, by which time it's mid-afternoon and all the restaurants are closed. We stop at a small supermarket where I buy a small bottle of sparkling Saumur wine, a couple of baguettes, some cheeses, and, remembering that Brad won't eat fresh fruit, a bar of chocolate, and some disposable cups and plates. We shelter from the heat in a shady part of the gardens of the château, tearing open the bread with our hands, and squishing cheese into it. It's a welcome opportunity to keep still for a short while. The nearby restaurant obligingly uncorks our bottle. Brad is uncertain about pouring good wine into a plastic cup, but other than drinking it directly from the bottle, that's our only option. The whole idea of eating with our hands, from our laps, is a novelty and an adventure for him. Once he has overcome his initial anxiety about the hygienic implications, he enters into the spirit of our picnic.

"This is how peasants eat," he laughs. It isn't the healthiest meal I've ever served, and it certainly isn't up to the high standards that he usually expects, but it is a very pleasant interlude, and Brad is the most relaxed and chatty he has been since his arrival. I see him as a small boy trapped inside the body of an elderly and introverted man compelled to rush through life in case he misses anything.

To digest and celebrate the success of our meal, we stroll around the gardens of Catherine de Medici, and Diana de Poitiers, maitresse en titre to Catherine's husband, and then we visit the interior of this prettiest and most feminine château. The relationship between Diane de Poitiers and Catherine de Medici is one of Brad's favourite topics, and he touches walls and doors where their hands may have rested, and looks from windows onto views that they would have seen. He isn't in a rush, and we spend three hours exploring the rooms, and savouring the experience of occupying the same space as once the two women had done. We are lucky to be there on a day when the crowds are thin, and we can move at our own slow pace without being hustled.

By the time we reach home it's after 10.00pm, we are both tired and Brad is leaving early the following morning. I make a simple omelette for dinner which he pronounces the best meal he's had since he arrived in this part of the world. I am enveloped in an aura of pride.

Next morning I drive him to town to collect the car he has hired for the rest of his holiday. He is driving back to Paris for a couple more nights, before heading towards Bordeaux to visit some of the great names in wine, and to continue his quest for fresh culinary and historical delights.

I feel quite depressed as I wave him away, because I am conscious that his stay has largely been a disappointment. I am not a chic, slick, elegant woman; my house is not a tasteful château, and the food everywhere has mostly been crap. Having spent three days with him, I have realised that he lives very much in a world of his own, and despite all our correspondence over the last few years little of what I have told him has sunk in. In his mind I have been a cordon bleu standard cook living in a historic and stately mansion with peacocks on the lawn, and looking like Catherine Deneuve. I imagine how much he must have anticipated his visit, and how disillusioned he must be feeling. Poor little man.

Today Ivy is splendid in scarlet harem pants and a matching bolero, her hair held back with a triangular scarlet chiffon scarf fringed with little dangling gold disks. She brings me a bin bag full of used clothing, as well as a battered cardboard box of various bits of china and old magazines. I already spend a silly amount of time clearing out unwanted junk, but she means well and I don't want to offend her. I'll take it to the charity shop next time I go to town.

Obsessively clean and tidy Brad has left no sign of his stay, and Lavande's guests are here for another week, so she only has to organise Pissenlit for new arrivals this afternoon. In no time at all she's finished and ready for a drink.

As she's knocking back a glass of rosé, she notices my new earrings, and comments on them.

"How pretty. Very unusual. Where did you get them?"

Absent-mindedly I mention Brad, explaining that he had spent three days here. Her eyes widen.

How long have I known him? Is he disgustingly rich? How did I meet him? What does my absent husband feel about me having a male visitor? Had he given me any other presents? How old is he? Has he been married? What does he look like? Where had we been? What had we done? What did we talk about? Is he coming back? She hurls questions like a knife-thrower.

I'm amused at her blatant nosiness. I don't know what makes me do this – I've never been any good at pretend - but I create a fantasy for her. I say Brad is a multi-millionaire with links to the Mafia. He wants to sever his links, and go straight, and plans to buy a château and convert it into an exclusive private hotel and restaurant. We have spent the last three days looking for a suitable place.

But the problem is, I continue, that once you're connected to the mob, they won't let you go. Brad is certain they're watching him, and that he's also under surveillance by the FBI. He sees his only way out is to quit the States and set himself up with a false identity in France, undergoing plastic surgery to change his appearance. He has the money to do so.

I watch carefully for any sign that she isn't swallowing my story, but her eyes are screwed in concentration, her lips are parted, and she keeps nodding encouragement.

He's in his early 60s, I say, a big man, very fit, tanned. Her head bobs harder and harder and the little gold discs tinkle. He's divorced, and we've been corresponding for two years.

114

Is there anything between us, she asks in a whisper. I open my mouth as if I'm going to confide in her, and then shake my head and bite my lip.

"I've already said too much – this wine must have gone to my head! But watch this space." I wink.

"Everything comes to she who waits," she murmurs.

She's quivering with excitement, and I imagine she can't wait to rush away and tell everybody who'll listen to her. I'm a cow sometimes. Still, I think she preferred my story to the boring truth.

I speed her on her way with an armful of glossy magazines, because I have a busy afternoon ahead. I am off to town to collect 12 dozen pink roses ordered a fortnight ago, and a bottle of pink champagne. I only have a single vase in the house, so I make a quick call to Tristram. By the time I return from town he has arrived with a car full of vases of differing shapes, sizes and designs, and he helps me arrange the roses. In tiny Pissenlit it's difficult to find room for them all. There are vases on top of the fridge, vases on the windowsills, vases on the draining board, vases on the floor, and even a vase on the cistern of the lavatory. Every available surface is covered in flowers. The fragrance is divine, and the place looks beautiful for our first honeymooners. I've put a small gift-wrapped box of Belgian chocolates into the fridge with the pink champagne.

Just after 4.00 pm the honeymooners arrive. Ted is as tall as Sarah is short, and she is as plump as he is thin, and they are standing at the gate, hand in hand, beaming. Sarah is a fountain of excitement, bubbling over with details of their flight from Philadelphia, the train journey from Paris to Poitiers, the car hire people who were so kind, and what beautiful little villages, and isn't the weather just too wonderful, it's like a dream come true, she can't believe she's here, can somebody pinch her - no, please don't - because if this is all a dream she never wants to wake up. She chatters on and on, and we are still standing at the gate.

"I just can't believe I'm really here in the heart of France! Ted said we were going to Florida, but when we got to the airport he kept turning this way and that, and then I saw we were getting on a plane heading to Paris. I've dreamed since I was a small girl about coming here, and now, at last, here I am. And with my wonderful husband."

She turns and smiles up at him. It's a long way from her 5ft (1.5 metres) nothing to his 6ft (1.8 metres) plus. Ted beams down at her, and when she finally pauses for breath he says in a lovely deep growl: "Silence, wife," and scoops her up in his arms. I lead them to Pissenlit, Sarah giggling, her arms wrapped around Ted's neck. Despite having to bend his knees almost to the floor to get through the doorway Ted manages not to drop Sarah, and puts her gently down. She gazes around in silence for a few moments.

"Oh my! This is too beautiful. It's just the cutest place you could ever dream of."

Then she sits down on the sofa and puts her face in her hands and sobs. Ted takes my hand in his two giant paws, and squeezes gently. It's a signal for me to retreat diplomatically.

When I take the dogs out this evening just before dusk, the honeymooners are sitting in their courtyard, holding hands and watching the sunset. I feel all gooey.

They've been here for two days, and I haven't seen anything more of them until Sarah knocks at the door to ask if I can let her have some baking powder, which she hadn't managed to find in the supermarket. She is cooking biscuits for Ted for lunch. Sounds like a strange lunch to me, but to each his own. And baking powder in biscuits? She's going to cook Ted's favourite dishes while they are here, in their first home as a married couple, she says, and she may need to borrow some pans.

Later she brings me a plate of biscuits, which are not what I call biscuits, but more like an English scone, which explains the baking powder. She's sweet and cuddly and still astonished to find herself here in the middle of the French countryside. Ted, she says, is the most gentle, beautiful man she has ever known, and she's the luckiest woman in the world.

Ted had contacted me at the beginning of the year to say that he and Sarah would be getting married in July. His funds were limited, but as his fiancée has always dreamed of visiting Paris and rural France, he is determined to make that dream come true. He sent payment for the cottage, including enough to cover the cost of the flowers and champagne, and asked me to book them into a good restaurant for their second night here. They will be staying in Pissenlit for five days. Sarah doesn't know yet that they will also be spending three days in Paris before flying home. And they say that the age of romance is dead.

When they aren't walking arm in arm, Ted sits in the courtyard smiling and pulling the dogs' ears, while Sarah rattles pots and pans in the kitchen. "I think I've made a good choice," he smiles. "I'll probably keep her. Fried chicken for lunch today." The happiness of these very gentle people makes me feel good.

"I don't know whether I'm more sad than happy, or more happy than sad," says Sarah on Thursday, with tears in her eyes.

"Ted just told me we're going to Paris tomorrow, and I'm so excited. But that means leaving this wonderful little place - our first home together. The first place we have lived under the same roof. You can't believe how happy we have been here."

While Ted is loading their bags into the car, Sarah stands watching him, holding my hand. "I really do love that man, you know," she murmurs. "Never did think this would happen for me. Not at my age."

I wave to them from the gate with a lump in my throat, watching two grey-haired people, one very tall, and one very short, as they drive slowly down the lane with a few little hoots, and then they are gone, onto their next adventure.

Over lunch earlier, I learned that Sarah had spent most of her life caring for her blind parents. Ted had been a widower for nearly twenty years when they met at a senior's club, and they married eight months later. Ted is 74. Sarah is 65.

The roses are still good, so I phone Ivy and ask if she'd like them. I don't personally like cut flowers – I prefer to see them living out their natural lives, not dying prematurely.

"You'll have to bring some buckets to put them in," I say.

She turns up with no buckets.

"Well, perhaps I could borrow the vases for a few days?" she suggests.

"No, you can't take them, because they're not mine. They're Tristram's."

She turns her lips down and wrinkles her nose. Ivy doesn't like Tristram.

This is a popular area for British immigrants attracted by low property prices, a benign climate - warmer and drier than northern France, and cooler than the south – with easy access to and from England by train, plane or road, and only an hour's drive from the Atlantic coast. The gently rolling hills are mostly given to arable farming, sparsely populated and with plenty of open spaces and uncrowded roads.

In an expatriate community the téléphone arabe - bush telegraph is never silent. There is a constant buzz of information flying in all directions. Hence I know a great many things of a delicate personal and sensitive financial nature about people I have never met, and probably never will. Fortunately these things tend to flow in one ear and out through the other within seconds, as I have very little interest in knowing about the misfortunes or scandals affecting my compatriots. But it is Ivy's daily bread. Give her a bottle of wine and a story of distress and she's on fire.

There are gay people of both sexes, transsexuals and a delightful transvestite – a slender, muscular, masculine builder with long wavy hair who wears earrings, nail varnish and lipstick at work and, at home, his wife's frocks and shoes. In Britain they probably wouldn't attract notice, but in an expatriate community in rural France nobody who deviates from what is regarded as the norm can slip under the radar. I relate to them the same as I relate to anybody – if they're nice, I like them. If not, I don't.

Ivy has only met Tristram once, when he and Beverly dropped in on their way to town while she was here working. They stayed ten minutes, and were chatty and charming, admiring her turquoise cheongsam. When they left, she sniffed and pulled a face. "Friends of yours?"

"Yes. Good friends. Very nice people."

"I hope you don't let them drink from your cups or glasses," she said. "You can tell from a mile away that they dance at the wrong end of the ballroom."

Today she has brought another bulging bin bag of things for me.

"All top quality," she says.

There are a couple of skirts with broken zips, two stained blouses, one also has a split seam, a weird multi-coloured satin garment, quilted and shapeless, I have no idea how it could be worn, and a pair of shoes bearing the footprints of the previous owner. All of them are a size smaller than me. I thank her and assure her that I now have sufficient clothing to last for the foreseeable future, and beyond.

Although I keep asking her not to bring any more "presents," she is not easily rebuffed, and a couple of weeks ago arrived with a cracked plastic garden table and a set of four tea-cups and three saucers that she thought I might like. "Waste not want not," she says.

Sometimes I can hear the proverbs before she's even spoken them. It's beginning to make me feel like stuffing a cloth down her throat.

Chapter Fifteen

Year Two – The Little People Who Live In The Hedge

TRISTRAM and Beverly have invited me for a lunchtime meal, and we spend a heavenly afternoon on the patio surrounded by scented flowers. We eat beneath a canopy of intertwined honeysuckle and jasmine, whose perfumes mingle on a slight breeze with the roses and lavender at the patio's edge. Beverly sprays the lavender with water to intensify its perfume, while the children snuffle around searching out and hoovering up crumbs. Beverly and Tristram are always excellent hosts, and it's about as perfect an afternoon as you could hope for. While Tristram adores his miniature Dachshunds, Beverly's passion is his garden, and he enjoys swapping cuttings and is kind enough to come over from time to time to use his expertise to keep our garden under control. I enjoy their charm, their intelligence, their kindness and most of all their togetherness and happiness.

Tristram is on top form, yodelling and singing. He and Beverly are off to Ireland for a fortnight on Saturday. His sister, her husband and children are coming to look after the dogs. Pansy whelped ten weeks ago, producing a litter of eight gorgeous puppies, bringing the headcount of Dachshund children to thirteen. Tristram is superstitious, and hopes it won't bring bad luck. The puppies are enchanting, and I could so easily have been tempted, but even with a "friends' discount" I could live for a year on what one of them would cost. It's the proceeds from the sale of the pups that is funding the holiday.

Our final guests for the year, an elderly couple, arrive at the end of September. Len is a tall dignified man, in trousers with a knife-edge crease, polished shoes, a white shirt and blazer. He shakes my hand and introduces Edie, a pretty woman dressed in pink, with startling blue eyes and a soft golden perm.

"How very lovely to see you again," she says, touching my face gently.

Len catches my eye.

"It's lovely to see you too, Edie. Let me show you the cottage."

In the living room, Edie says: "I'll just sort out these cushions. Yes." She moves the cushions around on the settee, and closes and opens the curtains.

"Len, take the other end of this um, take the other end so we can move it back." She lifts one end of the settee.

"Later, dear," says Len. "Let's sit down, and I'll make tea."

She sinks into the settee and puts a cushion on her lap. "There we are," she croons, stroking it.

"I'll leave you to it. Just give me a shout if you need anything," I say.

"We'll pick you up tomorrow," she smiles, holding up the cushion.

At the door, Len says, "You probably realise that Edie has dementia. But don't worry, she won't cause any trouble. I look after her."

"I'm sorry. It must be very hard."

"She's my wife. There's nothing hard about. It's my privilege to care for her," he smiles.

From the living room I can hear Edie talking on an imaginary telephone.

The weather is still dry and warm, and Len and Edie are out in the garden most of the day. Sometimes she walks round and round and round the same route, Len always by her side, always talking gently to her.

This afternoon there's a lot of shouting, and Len and Edie are by the car. He's trying to get her in, and she is running around the car yelling and hitting it with her handbag.

"I need to go shopping," he says, "but she won't get in the car. She's had a bad night."

So has he, I think. There are blue circles around his eyes.

"I can go. I need some things. If you let me know what you need, I can get it."

At the supermarket I look at his list, and see that amongst fruit, vegetables, meat and cheese he has asked for ten loaves of sliced bread, two pounds of butter and two pounds of ham. I wonder if tiredness has affected him, but I buy it all anyway.

Edie is in the garden picking grass. She's always immaculately dressed, her fingernails varnished, her hair brushed, and she's quite a beautiful woman. While Len is unpacking the shopping and putting it away, I sit with her.

"I've just phoned the police," she says. "I've told them what he's up to. He won't get away with it."

"Who?"

"Him. That man there."

"That's Len – your husband."

"Dirty man. He's got a brothel upstairs."

"I don't think he's doing that. He's putting the shopping away, and he's looking after you. He's a very nice man."

"Filling my house with prossies. Dirty fucker. The police will take him away again."

Len comes out with a tea tray and a large heap of sandwiches. He puts the tray down, gives Edie a cup of tea, and takes a handful of sandwiches and lays them under the hedge.

"More," calls Edie. "Make sure there's enough for the giraffes too. And put another fiver for the foreigners."

"What are the sandwiches for?" I ask.

"Those little people – all the immigrants living there in the hedge. You can see them – there, look - and the animals from the circus. And then you'll have to iron my clothes, you," she points at Len. "They're a mess. We're not going to see the – the things if my clothes aren't right."

Len lays a few more sandwiches beneath the hedge, kisses Edie on the forehead, and goes into the house and sets up the ironing board in the doorway of the kitchen, where he can see Edie. He brings down a heap of immaculately ironed outfits on hangers, and starts ironing them.

"I could do that for you," I offer.

"It's his job, that's where we get the money for the immigrants," Edie replies. She crumbles a Digestive biscuit, throws it up in the air.

Oh my goodness. How can anybody cope with this? How can you watch somebody all day long, and humour them without going round the bend? How you can watch somebody you love as their personality changes?

Len patiently irons all her clothes and hangs them up again, and I think how fortunate Edie is – if indeed you can regard anybody suffering from dementia as being fortunate – to have such a caring husband.

Before they leave, Len stocks up the sandwiches under the hedge. They're disappearing rapidly, I don't know what is eating them, probably the goats and chickens, but they're not going to waste.

After they've gone, I think a great deal about commitment. Sickness and health – does anybody imagine when they say those words that the future might hold decades of struggling to cope with a partner whose mind has moved on elsewhere?

Chapter Sixteen
Year Two – The Golden Goose

TODAY is Ivy's last session until we reopen next spring. Peeved that it's the end of the holiday season and her lucrative employment, she says she shouldn't have to put up with other people's filth, but I remind her that where there's muck, there's brass. Together we clean the place from top to bottom, storing away the linen, scrubbing the bathroom and kitchen, and covering all the furniture. She has bought some woollen crocheted cushions "to brighten the place up," and a picture of a tragic shepherdess clutching a frightened-looking puppy. She props it up on the mantelpiece between four plastic Fabergé eggs that have mysteriously appeared.

We spread dust sheets over the furnishings in Lavande, take down the curtains for cleaning and generally tidy up, then go around and check on anything that will need replacing for next year. Some people replace breakages extravagantly, others hide them. One guest left a cheque for €125 ($160) for a small stain on a mattress. Somebody else has burned a large patch on the dining table and covered it up with a mat.

There are some cracked glasses, chipped plates, a saucepan that has lost its handle and a couple of scorched table mats. A cushion cover is torn, and there are also various pieces of soap, tubes of toothpaste and hand creams. We scoop them all into a box for throwing away. Ivy searches every shelf and cupboard with the intensity of a child on an Easter egg hunt, and when we have finished I notice that a perfectly good bedside lamp has found its way into the box, which is now next to her car.

"I'll get rid of these for you," she smiles. "Save you going to the dump."

"Bless you. But I think this still has a bit of life left in it," I smile back, removing the lamp.

She's found an unopened bottle of Beaujolais in a kitchen cupboard, and pounces on it. "Let's knock this off, shall we?" she suggests, tugging the cork.

"So sad about that poor little baby," she starts describing some recent village tragedy I'd rather not hear about.

"What a fabulous outfit," I interrupt quickly. "Wherever did you find a gymslip? I didn't know they still made them. And your hair looks so pretty in bunches."

"So," she snaps suddenly – an unnerving habit she has - while I'm gazing in dismay at the cushions and picture, "what's the latest with Brad?"

"Who?"

"Brad. Brad, for heaven's sake!"

Crikey, how could I have forgotten about my relationship with Brad? She's looking at me very suspiciously.

"Actually, that's not his real name," I improvise. "It's only his cover. It's too early to say anything definite."

She snorts irritably. "It's taking a long time, isn't it? Are you sure he's still keen? There's many a slip between cup and lip."

I clench my fists to stop them wrapping themselves around her throat, then tap the side of my nose mysteriously. "No news is good news. Watch this space. By the way, is it true there was a shooting near your house recently?" I ask, skilfully diverting her.

Behind her bizarre appearance I see a lonely, friendless woman gazing at herself in the mirror in search of something she will never find, and it seems immensely sad.

She phones several times over the next few weeks – usually late at night and in a frenzy of excitement to report some appalling tragedy that she has heard of. A neighbour killed on a motorbike; a miscarriage; two divorces; a bankruptcy, and somebody taken into a mental hospital. While she chatters I play Mahjong on the computer, and say "Oh," "Goodness me," and "Really?" every so often, resisting the urge to say "Bad news travels fast".

Just as I'm getting used to days without interruption, the dogs announce an arrival. There's an auburn-haired woman in her early 40s standing at the gate, wearing a tartan mini-skirt, mustard-coloured woolly tights, chunky men's boots with big rounded toes, and a small strange cardigan fastened with bobbles of what look like small birds. Parked behind her is a gleaming black Mercedes estate car.

"Hi," she calls. "The Tourist Office told me you might have somewhere I could stay with my dogs for a few months."

She introduces herself: "Phyllis Crane, but everybody calls me Fliss. I've bought a farmhouse in La Petite Poterie," (a small hamlet not far from here.) "It needs loads of work doing, and I've got builders organised. But I need to be close to keep an eye on them. I don't trust these people at all."

I invite her into the kitchen and offer her a coffee, but after a glancing around, she says "No, thanks. I won't."

She tells me she's been living in Spain with her boyfriend, who has run off with an older woman. Luckily, she says, she owned their villa which she's now sold, and also has a private income from a trust fund. She's decided to move to France and "check out new pastures."

I show her around Pissenlit, pointing out that it's very small for a long term stay and that she'll have to get to grips with the log burner.

"Oh, I won't be here all the time. I'll be in Paris staying with a boyfriend most of the time. And I'll have to go England every couple of weeks to shop. The food's absolutely ghastly round here, you can't find any decent organic produce. This is just for when I come down to check out the progress on my renovations. As long as there's an Internet connection, and Pluto and Penelope can stay, that's all I need."

"And your dogs - I take it they're OK with other animals?"

"They both adore other dogs. They're really sociable. I promise they won't be any trouble at all," she assures me.

She'll rent Pissenlit from the beginning of November until the end of April. Before she leaves she writes a cheque for the full six months, and asks if I'll make sure that Pissenlit is properly cleaned before she returns.

Apart from a card to say that he was back in Oklahoma and to thank me for my hospitality, I haven't heard from Brad since he left. I feel sad to know that he was disenchanted with his visit here. What he'd think if he knew about his Mafia connections and our relationship I can't imagine. A sense of humour wasn't his greatest asset.

So it's a great surprise and delight to receive an email from him saying that his stay with me had been the adventure of a lifetime, and that he has some friends who want to come here next year. In his inimitably blunt manner, he says he has his doubts that they'll be very happy with the "primitive" conditions here, particularly as they have two young daughters and he thinks my standard of hygiene and safety – I think he was referring to the dogs and cats having free rein in the house – leaves much to be desired. But his friends have been inspired by his tales of rural French life and are very excited at the prospect of visiting, although he has warned them that I'm living almost in the Dark Ages.

When their email arrives, it isn't only a family of four who want to come and stay. Altogether there will be ten of them, family and friends, writes Annie, although not all at the same time. And they want to stay for eight weeks. With both cottages already booked from early June to the end of September next year, it's going to have to be the year after. Logistically I don't know how we will manage, but there's plenty of time to work it out. Meanwhile getting Pissenlit ready for Fliss and her dogs is my priority.

Ivy comes to bring Pissenlit up to the highest standard of cleanliness. She looks amazing today, with her hair pleated into a neat chignon knot at the nape of her neck and encased in a net. Of course she dyes her hair – at her age it isn't naturally golden blonde, but it's thick and lustrous, and really is her crowning glory. I ask her how she keeps it in such enviously glossy condition. She looks at me suspiciously at first but eventually admits that she uses lashings of coconut oil. I make a mental note to try that on my frizzy locks. She's gone horsey in cream breeches, long boots, a white shirt, a red tie with horses' heads sprinkled over it, secured with a gold tie-pin shaped like a folded whip, and a herringbone-patterned hacking jacket. All that's missing is a bowler hat, and a horse. Having rather short legs, the boots end up above instead of beneath her knees, preventing her from bending them, so she walks stiff-legged, as if her legs are made of wood. I try to imagine how she has driven her car here. Although she claims to be living in poverty, she has a vast wardrobe and I've never seen her wear the same outfit twice.

"Why does this woman want to stay here?" she asks.

I explain about the house renovation.

Ivy sniffs. "It sounds rather strange – she must have a particular reason for choosing La Petite Poterie. If she's that wealthy, I'd have thought she could afford to buy herself a home somewhere classy; more up-market. Like the Ile de Ré. Not in some dead-end place round here."

Ignoring the slur on our local area, which we love as do many thousands of other residents and visitors, I consider what she's said. In fact, despite the charm of this part of the world, La Petite Poterie doesn't immediately stand out as the kind of place a wealthy and fastidious woman would choose to live. But Fliss must have her own reasons for buying there, and it's no business of ours to question them.

Fliss phones to say she's been staying with her boyfriend in Paris for a few days, and will be coming this afternoon to check Pissenlit and test the Internet connection. Before she comes I double-check for dust and dirt, and air the place throughout. I don't want her changing her mind, because mentally I have already spent the money.

She arrives in her Mercedes, still wearing the tartan mini-skirt and big boots. In Pissenlit she gets a strong Internet and mobile phone signal, and is happy with the state of cleanliness. She asks me to order firewood for her and leaves cash to pay for it. As there is no washing machine in the cottage I say she can use our washing machine while she is here. She looks momentarily astonished, then explains that she always has her clothes professionally cleaned and will find a local laundry.

"I'll be driving down with my stuff over the weekend. Would you mind giving me my key now?"

I hand over the door keys. She clips them onto a fastening in her handbag as she climbs back into her car. Next day she phones to say that she's lost the keys. I have a new set cut and attach them to a very large chain.

It's 2nd November, bright and clear, with an easterly wind that could shatter marbles. Fliss arrived late last night; our dogs barked briefly, and I heard heavy footsteps over the gravel and a few canine yips, but I haven't seen her yet today. I'm huddled on a sofa wearing several layers of jumpers, three pairs of socks and a woolly hat and scarf, reading to take my mind off the cold, when a blood-curdling noise levitates me from the chair. It sounds as if all the fiends of hell have escaped and landed in the garden. I rush to the window to see a snowstorm of feathers flying round the lawn and our pet chickens hurtling in all directions, panic stricken. Two brindle whippets are chasing them in a frenzy of excitement, snapping and jumping at them. They catch one and shake it viciously.

"Pluto, Penny," calls a voice, weakly and ineffectually. "Bad babies. Come here. Naughty." The dogs takes no notice, drop the still body and set off in pursuit of another traumatised bird.

I leap out of the door as quickly as I can in my swaddled state, and scream at the top of my lungs: "STOP. YOU. FUCKING. HORRIBLE. ANIMALS."

Momentarily distracted, the dogs stop in their tracks and stare at me. The hens scramble into the trees and hedges. I grab Pluto by the collar as he wags his tail furiously. Penny dashes through the gate with her tail between her legs. A feathered body lies, stained red, motionless, on the grass.

"Oh Pluto, what a bad baby. You are naughty. Mummy is cross with you," croons Fliss, scooping him into her arms. I am rigid with rage and temporarily don't dare to speak for fear of slaughtering the golden goose.

"Bad boy," Fliss murmurs, rocking the squirming dog against her chest.

"I thought you said they were well-behaved," I say through tight lips.

"Oh, they are. I can take them anywhere and they've never been any trouble. Are you, baby? It's just that they don't like birds; they chase them. Oh, and rabbits. They do like killing rabbits. But honestly, they're absolutely fine with any dogs." She plants a motherly kiss on the dog's head and brushes away a couple of bloodstained feathers from its mouth.

We have two cats, and I can see that Pluto and Penelope are going to cause a major upheaval to our lives. Few dogs distinguish between a rabbit and a cat.

"You'll have to keep them on a lead while they're on our property," I say. "I can't have our animals being killed or terrorised. Don't let them into our garden again, please."

A crestfallen Fliss promises she'll keep her dogs under strict control and they won't create any more mayhem. She takes them back into Pissenlit and closes the door quietly. Next afternoon I find a beautifully wrapped box outside the door, with a small apologetic note attached from "Fliss, Plu and Pen". In the box is an oven-ready organic Bresse chicken. I stick it in the freezer until I can find somebody to give it to. It's not much use to a vegetarian. The bottle of wine I had left to welcome Fliss has been returned, with a brief note to say that she appreciates the gesture, but only drinks organic wines.

For a couple of days all I see of her is when she takes the dogs walking, always on the lead. Despite the bitter weather she's still only wearing the same odd ill-fitting outfit. She's a lonely figure, head bent, stomping along in the chunky boots. On an impulse, I ask her in for a cup of coffee. She puts Pluto and Penelope into Pissenlit, and returns with a small packet of green tea.

"Would you mind? It's organic produce. Have one yourself, if you like – it's terribly good for you." I decline politely. I loathe green tea.

Taking a scarf from her bag, Fliss wipes the table and the seat of the chair before she sits down, and the rim of her mug before she drinks.

Suddenly she lets out a shriek that makes me spill scalding coffee all over my chin, and she leaps up, knocking over her chair. One of our cats has jumped up on the chair next to her.

"This is Blackie," I say, scooping him up.

"Oh heavens, it looks so vicious," she gasps. "I think it wants to scratch me."

"He's not vicious. He's a pet." Blackie lies purring in my arms staring at her with feline contempt.

Fliss isn't convinced. "It looks evil to me," she says.

I think of Pluto and Penelope, who killed my chicken and who, according to Fliss regularly kill rabbits and birds – after all, they're only vermin, she says, and that's what dogs do - and I look at the black bundle that is too lazy to catch mice even if they sit under its nose.

"Don't worry," I say, "none of our animals are dangerous in any way. They won't hurt you." I put Blackie outside.

She's going away for a fortnight, back to Paris for a few days and then to England to stock up with "decent" foods. Would I like her to bring back anything? I say I'd be grateful for a jar of Marmite. She pulls a face. "All that salt! It's so bad for you." But she writes it down on her list. After she's driven away I find the list where it has fluttered onto the floor under the table.

I'm surprised to see her back here a few days later. She knocks at the door and asks if I have time for a coffee. Pissenlit is crammed with boxes of her belongings brought up from Spain, and there's no room for two to sit so she brings a tray round to the kitchen. I lock the cats away. On the tray is a little linen cloth, a cafetière, a tin of Fortnum's ground coffee, two elegant white china cups with a matching milk jug, and a plate of delicate little biscuits.

"They're organic," she says. "From Harrods."

The milk is organic, too. The coffee is very good, and so are the biscuits. Fliss gnaws at them with her two front teeth, like a squirrel. I notice that her eyes are a little red-rimmed.

"I was wondering," she says casually, "if you know any single men?"

A quick mental inventory finds five. Four French, of whom two are in their early 80s; one is terminally ill and one is a simpleton; and Luke who has done a few odd jobs for us.

"Is it for a friend of yours?"

"No, actually. It's for me."

"Oh, I thought you had a boyfriend in Paris?"

"So did I until I checked his mobile phone when he was in the bathroom, and found shedloads of photos and messages from other women. It means I'll be here most of the time now."

Poor girl. How demoralising so soon after her partner had left her.

"I'm terribly sorry," I say.

"Oh don't worry, I'll soon find somebody else," she shrugs. "I fully intend to."

I admire her spirit, but this isn't the best part of the world to hunt for eligible men.

"The only single man I can think of is Luke, and you definitely wouldn't like him."

"Why?"

"He's a lout, rude and rough. And he has a new woman just about every week."

"Oh, but I really go for rough types," she says quickly. "That's how I like them. Is there any way you could introduce me to him?"

Luke likes his women blonde, slim and young. Fliss is none of these. I say that he is often away, always busy, not very sociable, but Fliss is undeterred. "When I get back," she says, "you must get him round here so I can meet him." She's flushed with excitement.

Next day she leaves, two hours late because she's left the radio switched on in her car overnight and the battery is flat. By the time we've got it going she's lost her wallet containing her ticket for the ferry, and by the time she's found that (in Pluto's bed), it's obvious that she won't make the port in time.

"Don't worry," she says. "I'm always late for everything. You will speak to Luke, won't you? I'll be back on Tuesday."

While she's away, I phone Luke and ask him to come round next Thursday to repair some of our fencing. I'm quite sure it's a mistake.

Fliss returns late on Wednesday, having muddled up her dates and missed the return ferry. Her car is laden with cartons and bottles and packets, and she hands me a gift-wrapped a box of organic chocolates from Harrods. I notice that she's had her roots retouched. As I help her unload her car, she asks whether I've contacted Luke.

"Yes, he's coming over tomorrow mid-morning," I say.

"Oh great, I can't wait! Babies – guess what!" The dogs gaze into her eyes, ears pricked, tails wagging slowly. "Mummy's getting a new friend!" She claps her hands, and gives a little jump. I am enthralled by her self-confidence. "Come on – walkies!"

As she heads for the gate a car rattles up, and out climbs Ivy, looking uncharacteristically scruffy with her hair hidden beneath a scarf knotted under her chin and wearing a frayed track suit. Pluto and Penelope lunge towards her to say hello, scratching her with their claws and she almost falls over kicking out at them. Fliss drags the dogs away, calling apologies over her shoulder.

Without the pancake makeup, Ivy's skin is all lines and blotches; she looks haggard and old, and her breath is sour with red wine. She thrusts two bin bags at me. "Nice rugs for the gîtes, and some clothes for you," she says. "I scrounged them from some people who are going back to England." Nothing, it seems will deter her from bringing me things I don't want. The house is filling up with bed linen, curtains, odd bits of glassware and china, ornaments and pictures. She keeps giving the dogs bones, which constipate them, and has begun bringing clothes for my husband and grandchildren.

"I can't stop," she says, walking into the kitchen and sitting down, "but I'll just have a quick coffee. Terrible night; piles, can't stop the itching."

She flicks through my mail while the kettle's boiling.

"Who was that fat frump?" she snaps. "She let her bloody dogs rip my legs to shreds."

"That's Fliss – the woman who's staying in Pissenlit. Help yourself to a biscuit."

She studies the Harrods box.

"Where did you get these?"

"Fliss gave them to me. She goes to London every couple of weeks to shop."

Ivy's eyes light up. "Really? How useful. Well, sorry, I'd love to stay and chat, but I can't sit here all day. Tempus fugit. Must be off. I'm going to a funeral this afternoon. And another one tomorrow. In the midst of life we are in death."

From the kitchen window I see her fiddling about in her car until Fliss and her dogs return from their walk. She opens the car door and bends to stroke the dogs, and chats to Fliss for a few minutes.

"What a charming lady your friend is," remarks Fliss when I see her later. "She's invited me to lunch next week."

Luke turns up next day, with three German Shepherds. Whatever else, he is brilliant with his dogs. They are well-trained and never move further than a few feet away from him. Luke is his normal self: greasy-haired, reeking of tobacco, brown-toothed, black fingernailed. He wears a copper bracelet and several chunky silver rings. While we're looking at the collapsing fencing, Pluto and Penelope rush up yapping at the German Shepherds who are sitting beside Luke. Fliss follows, wearing an even shorter skirt than usual, and a plunging neckline despite the winter weather.

"Hi," she yells, catching her dogs by the collar.

Luke glances briefly at her, and then returns his attention to fence posts.

"I love your dogs," she tells his back. Luke ignores her.

"They're SO obedient. How do you make them like that?"

"I train them," Luke replies, scathingly.

"Oh, could you train mine? I could bring them over to you. What's your phone number?" Fliss has a pen and notepad in her hand faster than the eye can see.

Luke says he'll give me a call when he's worked out a price, whistles to his dogs, and walks to his car.

Fliss laughs "Wow! He's gorgeous. He's SO my type. I felt an instant connection between us."

I'm astonished, speechless.

She walks back to Pissenlit, humming and swinging her hips triumphantly.

November passes peacefully. Fliss is out most days supervising the renovations of her holiday home, or else back in England shopping. Penelope and Pluto have caused no more trouble.

Among our Christmas cards is one from James and Ellen, with a photo of a smiley, gummy baby John. There is also a card from Simon and Angela who stayed in Pissenlit on their house-hunting visit with her father, Alec. I'm very sad to read the enclosed note saying that Alec had died in the autumn, after a very long illness. He must have already been ill during their visit, when he slept with such fortitude on the dreadful futon.

Ivy by Elle Ford

Chapter Seventeen
Year Three – January

THE phone rings at midnight.

"Is your dear friend dead?" screeches Ivy.

"What? Who?"

"Her – that stupid woman staying there. Where is she?"

"Fliss? She's in England at the moment, I believe."

"Well, she was bloody meant to be here for dinner – I bought veal! Cost a fortune, and it's ruined. I've given it to next door's dog."

I say, "Oh dear."

She hangs up.

Fliss is very sweet, but she isn't at all reliable. She either forgets, mixes up the time or date, gets lost, or simply changes her mind. Probably many of us have done the same at some time. But the thing about Fliss is that she never apologises. I suppose she forgets that too. She's forever leaving on the radio or lights of her car and waking to a flat battery; losing her keys, her purse or her mobile phone, and spends half her time looking for things. I hinted that she should leave the spare door key somewhere in case she loses one. She puts it in the ashtray of her car before remembering she had locked herself out of the car twice in the last week (locking Pluto and Penelope in on one occasion) and had to call the garage out. Ivy puts it down to "needing a good seeing-to" and "that time in a woman's life when everything starts going downhill, tits, arse and little grey cells."

Chapter Eighteen
Year Three – Kiwis, Vet and Nuclear Cottage

OTHER holiday-home owners talk gloomily of bookings being down on previous years. However, I'm having to turn people away, because we are full every week from the beginning of June to the end of September. When the family from hell email to say they'll take Lavande for a fortnight in July, I'm able to reply truthfully that we are fully booked. However, some new holiday-home owners we know have failed to find any customers, so I pass the family from hell over to them. I'm happy, they're happy, the hellions are happy.

A couple of globe-trotting Kiwis telephone from England to ask if they can come and stay for a week. With Fliss and the whippets still occupying Pissenlit, I can only offer them Lavande, where there is no heating. They're not deterred when I tell them it's bitterly cold. They have cold weather gear, they say, and if I'd like a hand with anything, they'll be happy to help. Their one week turns into three, and in the end I don't charge them anything. They rough it in freezing temperatures – don't worry, they say, we're toughies – and they clear out the barns, muck out the horses, walk the dogs and generally make themselves useful. In the evenings they come to the house for a hot meal, entertain me with tales of their travels and drink extraordinary quantities of wine. When they leave they ask me to drop them at a motorway junction. They've no idea where they'll be going next. It depends on who stops to give them a lift and where to. That's how they are making their way around the world – spur of the moment decisions, footloose and fancy-free. A momentary pang of envy flicks through my mind.

Fliss says she has given up on Luke. She's been to his local bar and tried to chat to him, but he's pointedly ignored her. And she's driven round to his house and parked outside several times, and although his dogs barked wildly, he hadn't come to the gate. The fourth time she went there a young blonde came out and asked her to stop harassing them. She's decided to join a local expatriate group of singles and already has a date lined up for next week.

"He's not really my cup of tea," she says. "But it's better than nothing, and I just can't bear the idea that people think I can't find and keep a man."

There's not a lot I can say in reply, other than to hope that her date will be enjoyable.

Although she's in her early 40s, with her odd clothes and general dizziness I think of her as a girl, and feel quite protective towards her, as she seems very alone and vulnerable, and not really capable of looking after herself. This afternoon she came to show me the new dress she's bought for her date. It's the weirdest thing I've ever seen, pink and green zig-zag striped and shapeless garment, like a nightie, cropped at mid-calf length. With her money she could afford to dress well and make something of herself, and I wonder if she is trying to make a statement with her bizarre choice of clothes. I can't think of any other explanation. She must be able to see what she looks like.

When I wake early next day I see an elderly man leaving Pissenlit and walking as quietly as it is possible to walk on the crunchy gravel. However, when we walk our dogs together in the afternoon Fliss doesn't mention her date, and neither do I. She'll be moving into her house at the end of this month. We've become quite friendly over the last few months, and I've begun to realise that her life is an endless chain of catastrophes. From what she says the renovation work has been disastrous. She's not at all happy with the results and will have to employ more builders to put everything right. but she's philosophical. "I wouldn't expect anything less given my luck," she says.

Among our early visitors this year is Abbie, a lady vet and her boyfriend. She's traumatised by the mad cow and foot and mouth epidemics in Great Britain, and what she regards as the needless slaughter of hundreds of thousands of animals. Abbie is undecided whether to continue working as a vet, and the couple are taking a year to travel around the world while she considers her future. While they're here she gives all our animals a health check. Her experience shows in the way they are all relaxed as she opens mouths, examines feet, eyes and ears. She's surprised to learn that our mare Leila is nearly 40 years old, as she's as fit and sprightly, bright-eyed and glossy as a youngster. It's only her teeth that betray her true age. However, Abbie says that Cindy, our elderly chestnut Welsh cob, is showing signs of Cushings disease. Where Leila's coat is smooth and shiny, Cindy's is thick, woolly and coarse. She's suffered from laminitis for some years and needs special farriery. We know that her life is nearing its end, but she is still contented to mooch around grazing and sunbathing, and the two horses are inseparable. They were already old when we brought them to France, and some people had said it would be unkind to make them endure the long journey by road. In fact they stood up to it very well, and already enjoyed seven years of peaceful retirement here.

After a week searching in Brittany where it had rained all day every day, and another in the Loire valley where they couldn't find anything in their price range, Miles and Jess have arrived to have a look round the Poitou-Charentes. They are looking for a rural house with views, and are in the clutches of an agent who has set up a gruelling daily schedule of properties for them to visit. A couple of days ago they came back full of joy, having found a quaint stone cottage beside a stream. It has everything they want, and they can't believe it's been on the market for nearly a year without being snapped up. Tomorrow they're going to make an offer, and if it's accepted they'll sign the compromis de vente. The details show a chocolate box property with lavender shutters and a beautiful garden and lawn leading down to a stream. It seems suspiciously cheap, and when they show me on the map, I immediately know why.

"Did the agent mention the nuclear power station?"

They stare at me in horror.

"Where?"

"Just here. About four miles from the cottage," I point to the map.

"Jean-Paul didn't mention it," says Miles. "Are you sure?"

Dismay is written on their faces and I feel guilty at spoiling their dream. Plenty of people live in the shadow of the nuclear power station which was commissioned a couple of years ago. They probably didn't know they were going to when they bought their houses, though, as it isn't something estate agents regard as a useful selling point. At least Mike and Jess can make an informed choice.

Next morning they've reluctantly shelved the nuclear cottage, and are off to the Limousin to see another property over 60 miles away that sounds and looks idyllic from the details. But it's bad news when they return – it was a ruin. Three weeks of driving all over the country and getting their hopes up has only led to disappointment, and it looks as if they'll be going home on Saturday without having found their dream home. They set off on their last day, and are back in the early afternoon.

"Come with us! We think we've found the perfect place. Will you come and have a look?"

Ironically, after all the hundreds of miles they've covered, it's just one mile down the road from here, in the centre of the village, and not just one, but two adjoining houses. There's a lot of work to do, but both houses are attractive, solidly built and with some beautiful features, particularly the carpentry done by the previous owner, an artisan joiner. They've worked out that if they turn one of the houses into a holiday home, they can live in the other and enjoy an income, which will bring them closer to their dream of moving permanently to France.

Chapter Nineteen
Year Three – A Bicycle Made For Two

ONE afternoon while waiting for new arrivals, I hear a car engine pull up a little way down the lane, but nobody appears. Thinking they may have gone to the wrong house, I start out to investigate, and am greeted by a strange noise and most unusual and wonderful sight.

Around the corner appears a straw boater and a striped blazer; a flowery chiffon frock and a wide-brimmed straw hat decorated with flowers, astride a lovely old tandem bicycle. Honk, honk, honk, coming from a horn on the handlebars.

"We wanted to arrive in style!" calls out the man.

They look like a couple of film stars. He's lean, tall, tanned with a distinguished touch of grey at the temples of his black hair. She's slender and elegant, with long dark hair and a huge smile.

These kindest of people invite me to join them for a champagne supper. The practical, inexpensive glasses in Pissenlit don't do justice to Bollinger, so I bring over some of our remaining crystal. I've never met people so much in tune, so close, so completely right for each other. Joan has kicked off her shoes and is resting her feet in Michel's lap. He strokes them absent-mindedly, and bends to kiss her toes. Their story is the stuff of which great books are written, and great films are made.

When he was 18, Michel, who comes from a family of Belgian aristocrats, was sent to England to stay with relatives. He met Joan, one of his cousins who is the same age, and they fell in love. "It was," he smiles, "the great coup de foudre, (lightning strike)." For a year they were blissfully happy, and then Michel had to return home. He asked Joan to marry him. But Joan is Jewish and Michel is not. Joan's parents forbade her to marry a gentile.

"We were so young," says Joan. "I'd been brought up in a strict Jewish family. We were very close and the idea of disobeying my parents was unthinkable. They said if I married Michel, I would no longer belong to the family."

"I couldn't believe it when Joan said we couldn't marry," says Michel. "And yet they had let us go out together for a year. I asked Joan to come with me to Belgium, but she wouldn't leave her parents."

"Couldn't leave," she says.

"We were so sure that we belonged together. I was very angry. So hurt. I returned home, and broke all contact with Joan."

We sit in silence for a few minutes.

"We both had broken hearts," Joan continued. "I was certain I could never be happy with anybody but Michel. I wrote to him for a year, but he didn't answer. Eventually I met and married a nice Jewish boy."

"And I met and married a witch," Michel snorts. "A real, live witch. But I didn't know she was a witch until it was too late."

"And then?"

Many years passed. Although his marriage was unhappy, Michel would not leave the three children he adored. Joan and her husband parted amicably when he fell in love with somebody else. She remained single, running a successful business.

Many more years passed. Michel came to visit a relative in England. By pure chance, Joan was at the house when he arrived, and opened the door to him. The coup de foudre hit them instantly, as it had done almost forty years previously. This time, nothing would part them.

All their children were now adults, and independent. Michel had suffered from ill-health. He was working as a volunteer helping handicapped children. Joan would move to Belgium and live there with him.

It's a fairy tale.

But then Joan's husband, with whom she was still friendly, became chronically ill and bed-ridden. He and his partner had separated long ago. Now he's alone and unable to look after himself.

"There was nobody else who could look after him. The children have their work, and their own lives. He needs constant care. I felt responsibility for him. Michel agreed."

She smiles at him.

"And so we worked out a compromise. Every month, I stay with my husband for two weeks and look after him. And then I spend two weeks with Michel, and my husband has live-in carers while I'm away."

"How long has he been ill?" I ask.

"Four years. And now you wonder how long he might live," she says astutely.

"It could be another twenty years."

"And you and Michel will not mind?"

"I would expect no less of Joan," says Michel. "I am so proud of her. And every time we see each other again, we have a new love affair. It's wonderful. Our time together is so special because it is limited."

What an amazingly beautiful couple they are. I think theirs is the most touching and romantic story I've ever heard.

Chapter Twenty

Year Three – Must Read More Carefully

IVY has crashed her car and is without transport, so I have gone to collect her. When I arrive at her gloomy little house (the Black Hole of Calcutta, as one acquaintance calls it), in a grey back street of a nearby town, there's no sign of life. I knock, and then bang on the door, then the windows, but she doesn't answer, although I'm certain I can hear noises indoors. I go and sit in the car, to wait a while to see if she'll appear, and while I'm sitting there, an old lady taps on the window.

"Are you looking for the English woman?" she asks, jerking her head at the house.

"Yes. She said she'd be here, but there's no answer. Do you know if she's OK?"

Over her shoulder appears the face of an old man.

"Ha! OK?" he snorts.

"Shh," says the old lady. "She's not well. They have put her to bed."

"What has happened?" I ask.

The old girl hesitates, but he jumps in.

"She was walking around half naked, shouting. She stepped in front of the postman's van and he nearly knocked her down. She tried to get in with him. She was wearing only a nightdress. And making a lot of noise."

The old lady listens anxiously, nodding her head in agreement.

"The postman tried to take her into her house, but she screamed at him – struck him. She was very violent, very rude. Those people," he pointed to the next door house, "came out, and so did the English people who live on the corner. We all had to hold her and take her into the house. Then the English people stayed for a while. When they came out, they said she was asleep." He spat on the ground, and put a fist to the end of his nose, twisting it, the French sign for drunkenness. It was only 10.30 in the morning.

"No," I say, "perhaps she's ill? Maybe she needs a doctor."

"Forgive me, Madame, if she is your friend, but this is not unusual. She is often drunk, in the day and in the night. Sometimes she lies down in the road and stops the traffic. It isn't the way we behave here." He shakes his head, and the two of them toddle away.

I scribble a note and stick it to her door, saying that she should give me a ring when she can. Then I go home and grudgingly start the cleaning myself. The phone rings just after 1.00, and Ivy announces that she has fully recovered and would like to be collected. For once she's dressed appropriately for the work ahead – shell suit bottoms and a T-shirt. Her eyes are red-rimmed and red-veined, her face puffy and blotchy, and her hair wrapped in a bulky towelling turban. I ask if she's sure she feels well enough to work, and she says that yes, the antibiotics work very quickly.

"Migraines," she explains. "I'm a martyr to them." Antibiotics for a migraine?

"Oh," I say, nodding sympathetically, "how dreadful for you."

"I'll probably be brought down by them at least once a week," she forecasts.

"I hope it won't happen on Saturdays," I mutter.

After the mix-up of bookings in our first year, I thought I'd learned to read my emails more carefully, but events this week make me realise I have a way to go. This afternoon both sets of guests arrive simultaneously. The couple who have booked Pissenlit have been involved in a minor car accident recently. He has an inflatable sausage around his neck and she has one arm in a sling so I concentrate on settling them, leaving Lavande's guests – a trio of naturalists as they had mentioned in an email – to sort themselves out.

"Do feel free to wander around the field," I call. "There are loads of wild flowers, and you might see some lizards and snakes. Also the hoopoes are around at the moment."

Later, while I am dead-heading the roses, a voice calls from the other side of the hedge.

"Hola! Fancy popping round later for a drink at 6'ish?"

"OK, thanks, I'd love to."

Armed with a bag of books on wild flowers, birds, reptiles and insects, I'm a little non-plussed when a naked and, as I can't help noticing, exceptionally well-endowed man opens the door and ushers me into the kitchen.

"Am I too early?"

"No, no. Not at all. Come on through."

He leads the way to the patio, where two ladies are sprawled on sun loungers wearing nothing but sunglasses and straw hats.

"Right, introductions. Linda, my wife, Sacha, our sister-in-law and I'm Richard. Gin and tonic?"

He guides me to a chair and hands me a chilled glass embellished with a slice of lemon and audible bubbles.

"Santé!"

The ladies are well away already, feeding gin-soaked slices of lemon to our chickens. It all seems rather surreal and I feel distinctly overdressed.

None of them seem very enthusiastic about the books, but thank me politely. Suddenly I have a eureka moment.

"You're not naturalists, are you?"

"Heavens no! What gave you that idea?"

"I misread your email."

An hour later I'm as drunk as I've ever been in my life, and wobble back to the house with my bag of books, feeling rather foolish.

Chapter Twenty-One
Year Three – Cut-price Customers

A gruff voice phones and asks how cheap I can do Pissingly for him. I tell him that the rates are on our website. "Aye," he says. "I've seen them, but what I want to know is, what price is it for me and the wife?"

It's the same for everybody, I reply.

"Rubbish. Only a fool won't make a deal with a keen customer," he says. "You give us the right price, and you've got a deal. Me and Melanie are pensioners, we can't afford your fancy prices."

I tell him that not only are our prices as low as he is likely to find anywhere, but that Pissenlit is fully booked for the whole season. That knocks the wind out of his sails, and he changes tack.

"Well, we'll take the other place then at the same price as Pissingly."

"Look," I said, "I really am sorry, but there isn't anything I can offer you. We don't have any vacancies."

"So we'll not be having a holiday," he says, mournfully. "And I'd promised Melanie I'd take her away this year."

I advise him to book something in advance for next year, and he hangs up, but not before leaving his phone number "in case something comes up."

And strangely enough, it does a couple of weeks later.

An extremely nice man has taken Pissenlit. James has written a book and wants a quiet week to give it a final edit, as he has to have a complicated operation on his hand in a few weeks' time, after which he'll be unable to type for a couple of months. I invite him in for supper when he arrives, as he's alone, and we spend an enjoyable evening discussing writing and our reading tastes, which are very similar. James does not have a mobile phone, and had asked if I would mind if he gave my landline number to his son should he need to contact him. Next afternoon there's a call for James. He comes to the patio, shaking his head.

"I've been waiting almost a year for my operation. Now they decide to bring it forward to the day after tomorrow. I'll have to leave straight away! I don't believe it. What a bummer."

While I help him load his things into his car, he refuses my offer of a refund. "I'll be back one day," he smiles. "I'm in credit with you."

It's when I'm tidying up in Pissenlit that I remember Mr Gruff.

If I expect him to be thrilled and overflowing with gratitude when I phone to say he can have Pissenlit for five days, I'm delusional. What about the cost of travelling at the last minute? It's going to cost a fortune! After listening to many minutes of wailing and wheedling, I agree that he can have five days for the price of three, for which he will pay cash on arrival. When I put down the phone I feel worn out, and rather guilty at charging them anything since James had already paid in full.

They arrive in a noisy battered old car. He has a small reddish moustache and a large reddish face, and is wearing a pair of ladies' spectacles with a winged purple frame. He reminds me of a well-loved, threadbare teddy bear. His wife is short, plump and timid, and walks two paces behind him.

I show them into Pissenlit. "Ee, it's a bit on the pricey side for what it is," says Teddy-bear. "What we'll do, pet, is pay you when we leave. Like you do in a hotel."

We are not a hotel, I say, and with some difficulty extract from him the measly amount I'm charging. They should let me know if there are any problems, I say. I'm fairly sure there will be.

Not five minutes have passed, and there is a hesitant tap at the door.

The little wife is standing there, flushed and on the verge of tears. She thrusts the welcome pack at me. "Harry said I should bring it back. We've brought our own food with us."

Behind her Harry yells: "Have you given it back? Tell her we're not paying for things we didn't order."

I take the basket from her. "It's a welcome pack. Just a few things to make you feel at home, that's all. It isn't meant to offend."

"It's a gift, Harry," she calls.

"And I suppose she includes it in the price of the rent," he shouts.

I call back, "It's a gift. It's free. With my compliments. But you don't have to have it if you don't want it."

Harry marches briskly over the gravel, his round face one huge smile. "Well, in that case," he takes back the basket, "we'll keep it."

"What I don't like, you see, is being ripped off. And these frogs certainly know how to do that. They're bloody crooks, the lot of them. Melanie will tell you," he pushes his chin towards his wife. She wrings her hands nervously.

I take a deep breath.

"I think you'll find the people round here very friendly and honest," I say pleasantly.

"I doubt it. I've never known a frog you can trust. Nor a spic. They're all thieving bastards," he calls over his shoulder as he stomps away, Melanie following obediently.

Ten minutes later, he's back, waving the bottle of rosé I had put in the fridge for them. "Could we change this for some beers, pet? Only we don't really drink wine. Or if you give us the money, we'll buy some beers ourselves."

"Of course," I say graciously, opening my purse and digging out €2 ($2.50), which I hand to him. He looks at it suspiciously. "Eee, that's not much. Are you sure?"

"Yes," I reply. "It wasn't a grand cru." I think that's lost on him.

He grunts and pockets the coins.

Melanie stands just behind him, looking as if were the ground to open up and swallow her, she'd be relieved.

"There's a bakers and small grocery in the village, a mile down there," I point to the road.

"We'll not be needing bloody supermarkets. We've plenty of food with us. Good English food at honest English prices. We don't eat foreign muck."

I wonder why they've come to France for their holiday.

"Then you probably won't be eating out while you're here?" I ask.

"Are you daft, or something? At the prices they charge here? What do you think I am, a plum pudding?"

I give up, and leave them to unpack half a dozen Tesco shopping bags from their car.

It's a mild evening, and the nightingales are singing. I'm sitting outside when I hear a cough. Harry is standing behind me, with a couple of bottles of beer in his hand.

"Do you mind if I sit down, pet? Have a beer with you?" He passes me one of the bottles and takes a chair next to me.

"I've never heard birds singing in the night," he says.

"They're nightingales. I'd never heard them until I came to live here. They come here from the south during the summer to breed."

"That's a beautiful sound. And when you look up and see the stars, that's all you need, isn't it? You don't need to be spending money going out, or having a television. Like the song says, the best things in life are free, aren't they?"

We sit silently for a while, and then he says: "You probably think I'm a tight bastard."

I say nothing.

"And I am. I know I am. I can't help it. I've got plenty of money, and I know I can't take it with me, but I just hate spending it. I keep telling meself that I'm going to

160

change, and start enjoying life, and give Melanie a real treat, like a world cruise. But there's something stops me all the time."

After we've finished our beers, he stands up. "Well, goodnight, pet. I've enjoyed talking to you." He takes two paces, then turns around. "Mind you, when I'm gone, Melanie will be a rich woman. She knows that."

"But wouldn't she rather enjoy the money with you, now?"

"Of course she would. But I've told you – I just can't bring meself to spend it. Anyway, she wouldn't know what to do with it. She's a good woman and a wonderful cook, but she's not the sharpest knife in the drawer." He shakes his head. "It's the way I am. I think it's an illness."

As he wanders back to Pissenlit, I feel like a priest who has heard a confession but doesn't know what penance to hand out.

Each day the two of them drive away, late morning, with their Tesco carrier bags, returning to spend the afternoon sitting in the sun reading. I see almost nothing of Melanie, but in the evenings Harry comes over to sit with me in the dark, looking at the stars and listening to the birds of the night over a beer.

He jokes: "You don't know how lucky you are – not many people can say I paid for their round."

I laugh. I can't help liking him.

"Wouldn't Melanie like to come and sit out here, too?" I ask.

"No," he says, "she's indoors knitting. She loves knitting. She knits presents for friends and family. Toilet roll covers, dolls, scarves. She's a marvellous knitter, and very sharp at finding cheap wool. And it gives her something to do in the evening. We don't have a telly – not with the wicked cost of a licence nowadays."

On the eve of their departure, I ask if they've enjoyed their stay. Melanie nods enthusiastically, and Harry puts a hand on my shoulders.

"Pet," he says, "we've had a grand time. I think you're overcharging, but I'm not going to complain because you're a nice person. We found a lovely spot for our picnics – less than five miles away. With the wicked price of petrol we're not going to waste it driving for miles. Melanie boiled up a couple of frankfurters on our little camping gas stove, and we popped them into bread rolls, and it were champion. Then we brewed up a nice pot of tea. What more could you want for a good day out?"

I'd want quite a lot more, actually, but I don't want to seem greedy.

"You said you didn't eat foreign food," I reminded him. "Frankfurters are German."

"You're kidding me. I thought they were English." He mulls this information over for a few seconds. "Well I'll be damned."

"Do you know," he continues, "that we only spent £20 ($30) on food to bring with us, and we've still some left for the journey home."

"Well, that's pretty good. But don't you eat in the evening?"

"We have Pot Noodles when we're on holiday. Just boil up the kettle, and there you are. A meal in minutes. And a spot of tinned fruit with evaporated milk. Now, pet, I was going to mention that as we haven't used any gas, and perhaps you'd like to give us a little refund?"

"Harry, sod off."

He laughs. "You don't blame me for trying though, do you?"

He chuckles his way back into Pissenlit, and by the time I've woken up next day, they've left.

The little cottage is spotless and has been thoroughly cleaned out. There's not a speck of dust, a single crumb. There's no kitchen or loo rolls, cleaning products, or light bulbs in the two bedside lamps. And for once, there is no half-pot of pepper or partly-used jar of jam.

Even the pen that was attached by a string to the guest book has vanished. I smile and shake my head. It takes all sorts.

Chapter Twenty-Two
Year Three – With The Best Of Intentions

IVY is becoming very proprietorial, referring to "my domain." She wants to know everything about incoming and outgoing guests, what they did, where they come from and what I thought of them. I find a handwritten notice sprinkled with golden glitter, blue-tacked to the door in each of the lavatories:

TOILETS MUST BE CLEANED AFTER EACH USE. BY ORDER.

Like her namesake, she is slowly squeezing her tendrils into our lives. She doesn't clean all that well, but better than I do, and when she has gone I have to go and sweep down the cobwebs that she has missed, but it isn't arduous and I don't mind.

Today she has brought two single duvet covers and matching pillow cases that she found at a car boot sale, a cardboard box full of cheap ornaments, and a couple of slightly grubby rugs.

"I thought our cottages could do with some brightening up," she explains. "Make them more homely."

She flaps the rugs down on the living room floor in Lavande, and adds to the collection of plastic Fabergé eggs on the mantelpiece. Then she drags all the furniture around into what she says is a better layout. Recently she has begun to extend her empire into our house. I've found a trio of wooden monkeys sitting on the mantelpiece, and a hand-embroidered tablecloth on a side table. I might as well admit it: I am terrified of losing her, because I know that the chances of finding a replacement are next to zero. So I smile meekly and weakly at the assorted and unwanted stuff and do my best to keep her in a good mood, although I do have to insist she takes down the string of fairy lights she has festooned around the mantelpiece of Lavande. Maybe nearer Christmas, I say. Not in mid-summer.

Being a coward, and even worse being dependent upon her to save me from the horrors of the mop and bucket, vacuum cleaner and duster, I humour her as far as possible. Such is her power over me that during the summer I rush around after she has cleaned, and hide some of the dreadful things, then put them back again when the guests have left and before she arrives. It's a totally ridiculous state of affairs, but unless and until I can find somebody to replace her, I do it to keep her happy.

Her relentless questions about my fantasy relationship with Brad have nearly driven me mad. I've strung her along for several months, saying that "things are happening behind the scenes." Today she starts to recount with relish the tragedy of a local French man who blasted his ex-wife and their daughter to death with a shotgun and then killed himself. Interrupting a description of writhing agony and spattered gobs of flesh, I say, "I've heard from Brad."

I hand her a photograph of a total stranger I have downloaded from the Internet. Bearing a strong resemblance to George Clooney, he is leaning against a gleaming convertible Mercedes. I have scrawled on the back in wild writing: "One day ……… L." And there's a flamboyant heart pierced with an arrow beneath the scrawl.

That's crafty, you see. I'd remembered saying that Brad wasn't his real name when she caught me out all those months ago.

She's temporarily dumbstruck, staring from the photo to me and back to the photo.

Then with a snort she flicks it back to me, muttering something about handsome is as handsome does. She looks highly irritated, and I smile inwardly. As smart as she is, she's easily taken in. Perhaps she'll drop the subject now. I hope so, because I don't know where to steer my relationship with Brad. I'm not going to give her the satisfaction of thinking he dropped me! At the same time, I'm appalled that I'm using his name in such a deceitful way. I can't imagine what he'd think if he knew.

Long-standing friends are getting married in England in August. With the animals and guests, it's going to be difficult for me to get away unless I can find somebody very reliable to take care of it all. When I mention this to Ivy, who is wearing a colourful Pierrot costume today complete with conical hat and pompom, she volunteers to move in and "take over the reins" while I'm away. My mind goes into freefall at the thought. She isn't very keen on the dogs and knows nothing about horses, so I respond with a quick lie (I notice with dismay that this is only one of a long chain of lies that I've told her). "Bless you, how kind. However, I have already found somebody to come and stay. We need someone very strong and good with horses – they are terribly vicious at this time of the year, because of the horseflies."

She looks at me a little suspiciously, but I manage to meet her gaze without blinking or blushing, mentally apologise to our two horses who are as gentle as baby mice, and set about searching for a suitable somebody.

When I come across the following advertisement on a French forum, it looks as if it could be the answer to my prayers.

"English lady, animal lover, early 50s, available to house/pet-sit, or as working guest. Experienced with horses. Honest, reliable, non-smoker. Full driving licence. References on request."

I ask the advertiser for references, speak to two people who assure me that Alison is a treasure, and arrange that she will come and stay for about a month, spending a week here before I leave so that she can get used to the routine, covering the fortnight I'll be away, and giving her time to find somewhere to move on to once I'm back.

Dynamic is an understatement where Alison is concerned. She's like a human hurricane. Her motto is "Elbow grease, enthusiasm, energy, efficiency." She's up every morning at daybreak, turfing the dogs out of their beds so she can hang their blankets out in the sun. She's banging in some fence posts that look in danger of falling down. She's smeared Vaseline around the horses' eyes and nostrils to keep the flies at bay. She never stops.

I heave myself out of bed at an uncustomary 7.30 am, feeling guilty for being such a slugabed while I can hear the vacuum-cleaner purring. Breakfast is set out on a tray in the garden. We are using a teapot. I could get used to this, but it is not what I was expecting.

"There is no need for you to work like this. You're not here to be a slave. Why don't you just sit and read, or sunbathe, or go for a stroll?" I ask.

"Never! I would hate it. I have to move, be on the go, all the time."

She jumps up to dead head some roses with the secateurs that she carries permanently in her pocket, then goes to check the horses for ticks and to spray them with the special anti-fly lotion she makes up. This afternoon, she says, when it's too hot to be outside, she'll be re-organising cupboards and cleaning mirrors.

Alison has a cut-glass accent but a very down-to-earth, slightly brusque manner and a weather-beaten appearance, with scrubbed skin and cropped hair. She's slender and fit, uses no cosmetics, and says that soap and water is all that skin and hair needs. I'm curious to know more about her, and when I can get her to sit still for a while, I learn that she's always "done her own thing" since she left school. She'd been a chalet girl, run her own recruitment agency, travelled all over the world, lived in Australia on a ranch, worked as a PA. Whatever she does, she gives 100%. She's enigmatic about her personal life, saying that she prefers animals to people. She has no family, and owns no property, preferring, as she says, a life free of shackles.

Under her seemingly brittle exterior she is warm and funny. The animals all love her and are very much more obedient to her than to me. The house and garden are in shock, recoiling from dusters and brushes and lawnmowers; burgeoning weeds shrivel and retract beneath the ground at the sight of her. Alison is clearly enjoying herself, whistling and singing as she goes about her self-appointed chores. She's easy to feed, happy to eat vegetarian, and enjoys a few glasses of wine.

Once the guests have checked out on Saturday morning I show her where to find stopcocks, spare bulbs, how the gas works, and explain that Ivy will come to do the necessary cleaning. I will leave her money in an envelope with Alison, who is completely confident that she'll have no difficulty in dealing with any situation that might arise. She suggests that we don't need Ivy for the two weekends I'll be away, because she'll happily manage the changeovers herself. No, I say, explaining that Ivy rather depends on the income and we don't want to do anything to upset her.

When she arrives today Ivy is dressed as a flamenco dancer, with multi-coloured satin frills and Cuban heels, and a large tortoiseshell comb pinning a mantilla to her glorious locks.

"Oh my giddy aunt," murmurs Alison.

I introduce them. Alison says "How do you do?" and without any preamble Ivy snaps,

"Are you terribly good with vicious horses?"

Alison looks momentarily taken aback – I hadn't mentioned Ivy's offer to house-sit - but says, yes, she was virtually born in the saddle and can handle any equine behaviour. Ivy sniffs and says that's OK, then.

"Now I must leave you two ladies of leisure to relax and enjoy yourselves whilst I get on with the menial work," she adds sourly. Alison raises her eyebrows.

When I leave the following Thursday I do so with a light heart, confident that Alison will keep everything under control. She has copious notes covering every imaginable eventuality, and my mobile phone number in case of emergencies. I call her a couple of times and she assures me that everything is running like clockwork, the animals are all fine, and so are the guests. She has had to have a little word with Ivy, whose cleaning, she feels, isn't very thorough, and has reminded her to wipe all the door handles and taps. She was certain she could smell wine on her breath, too. "Don't worry, though. I went round and cleaned properly once she'd gone."

"Please don't upset her," I say. "It's impossible to find cleaners. I don't want to lose her."

"Well, you can't afford to be weak with people like that," Alison replies. "They'll only keep taking more and more liberties. You do have to be firm so that she understands that she works for you, and that you're the boss. Frankly, I don't think she's up to much."

When I arrive back home late on a Sunday evening, the house and garden are pristine, the animals groomed, fed, obedient and happy, supper is on the table, and the wine chambré. I can see lights on in Lavande, but Pissenlit is in darkness. Alison says that everything has been fine during my absence, there had been no problems, and so, after a very long day, I go to sleep with a light heart.

Next morning we are breakfasting in the garden, while Alison simultaneously tugs embryonic weeds out of the cracks in the patio. I ask idly if Saturday's changeover had gone smoothly, and she says yes, it was fine. Ivy failed to turn up, so she'd cleaned the cottages herself – properly, and not before time. Had Ivy phoned, I ask.

No, apparently not. That sounds rather ominous.

There doesn't appear to be anybody in Pissenlit. Haven't they arrived yet?

Yes, Alison said, they did arrive, but left almost immediately without explanation.

I phone their home number, but there's only an answering machine.

There is a small pile of mail stacked neatly on my desk, and nothing of great interest, apart from a handwritten envelope containing a picture of a bunch of flowers cut out from a magazine, glued to a piece of card and sprinkled with sequins, with a curt message from Ivy to say that she is no longer available.

Again I phone Pat and John, the people who had booked Pissenlit, but there is still no answer. I try again on Tuesday, but am still unable to contact them. Why they left so suddenly is a complete mystery. Alison is as puzzled as I am.

On Wednesday the postman arrives bringing a recorded delivery envelope bearing a scathing missive from Pat and John, who write to say that they are outraged by the reception they were given, and fully intend to take every possible step to publicise their treatment to ensure that as many people as possible are warned against staying here. I can't believe what I'm reading.

"What exactly happened when they arrived?" I ask Alison.

"I went to greet them. They seemed very friendly - but they were both men."

"Yes. And?"

"Well, I said I thought there was a mistake, because Pissenlit only has a double bed. I said that I would see if the couple in Lavande would be prepared to swap with them, because the second bedroom has two single beds."

"They just looked at each other and picked up their bags without saying a word, and got into their car and drove away."

"Oh dear," I say. "That wasn't terribly tactful."

"What do you mean? Did I do something wrong? I thought I was being helpful."

"Of course you did, but it sounds as if they were gay, and you offended them."

She looks blank.

"But surely they wouldn't want to share a double bed?"

"Yes."

"Oh lord, I just thought they were brothers, or friends. I must have upset them pretty badly. I'm dreadfully sorry."

She sits crumbling up her cake and swirling her tea around in the cup for a few moments, then says briskly, "Well, what's done is done. No good crying over spilt milk. I've certainly learned a lesson. Good heavens. Now, a change of subject. I made a terrible discovery while you were away. Those people who live at the end of the lane are mistreating their animals very badly. The poultry had no water, and the dog was on such a short chain. They went away for two days and left them all without food or water."

I nod. The people are notorious for their disregard for the welfare of their animals, but in rural France neighbours are like the three wise monkeys, and most particularly they don't make complaints against each other. I've talked to the other neighbours and asked them what we can do, but they say there is no point in complaining, because nothing will be done. When I spoke to the mayor, she said this was the country, and country people have a different view of animals.

"I'm afraid it's the French way in this part of the world. They're not sentimental about animals."

Alison flushes angrily. "For God's sake, I've lived in India and Africa, where animals are mistreated as a matter of course because of ignorance, but what I have seen here is worse than any Third World country. These people know better, but they just don't care. Anyway, I went to see the Maire, and I've contacted the gendarmes."

Over the next three days we have visits from the Maire and his assistant, four gendarmes, and two veterinary officers. They all examine the animals in question, decry the conditions in which they are kept, and produce clipboards full of forms to be completed. In confident but slightly garbled French, Alison berates them and tells them they'd be better employed removing the animals than filling in paperwork. The visitors confer amongst themselves and leave, promising that we will hear from them within 14 days.

By which time Alison has left for her next adventure, escorting a handicapped old lady from London to New Zealand, something that I know she will do very well indeed.

Although she leaves behind her a cauldron of turmoil as a result of her genuine naïveté, dedication and sense of what is correct, I don't hold any of it against her. She's welcome here any time, and I'd trust her with everything that is dear to me.

Following visits from the authorities, the neighbours are censured and ordered to tidy up the filth in which their animals, and they themselves, are living. They glare sullenly at me whenever our paths cross. We will remain enemies for life.

I write a note to Pat and John, apologising for any misunderstanding and offering them a refund. There is no reply.

Fortunately for the next couple of weeks our guests all leave the cottages clean and tidy, leaving me little to do and saving €30 ($40) a week, and I feel I can cope well enough with any cleaning.

Late one evening the phone rings. "Well?" shrieks a familiar voice.

"Yes thank you. I'm fine," I reply, unhelpfully.

"What is happening? Why haven't you called me?"

"You wrote that you weren't available any more. I have managed to cope without you."

"How extraordinarily clever of you. Bravo! So you are now superwoman and have learned to do what any normal woman does as a matter of course. And having done so, you have decided to cast me onto the rubbish heap like an empty bottle, despite two years of devotion to duty. Well, never mind, then, it will be best for everybody if I just die. You'll all be delighted. Let me simply starve, and the cats eat my body. Better that than trying to survive living on the streets. You snotty bitch, I hate you. Oh Jesus, why doesn't anybody care about me?"

I realise then that she's very drunk. She starts sobbing, and I try to think of something to say. Don't give in, I tell myself. Stand firm.

"Please," she whimpers, "please." Now she's really crying, and hiccuping.

I say, "Well, if you could come next Saturday at the usual time, I'd be so pleased."

She sniffs. The sobs stop instantly. "Right," she hisses, and the phone is slammed down. I feel like slapping myself in the face.

She's uncharacteristically subdued when she turns up on Saturday morning wearing a tailored grey wool suit with a corsage of orchids pinned to her left shoulder, and a grey felt hat with a maroon ribbon around it. She is smothered in make-up, and looks like a cross between a Salvation Army officer off to a wedding and a St Trinian's girl at the 50th anniversary reunion. She knows she might be skating on thin ice after her recent rudeness, and, remembering Alison's advice, I'm a little cool, just to remind her who's boss.

After she has driven away, scraping the fence post, I notice that crocheted dolls have appeared on the toilet rolls, and a row of Russian dolls on the mantelpiece in Lavande. I wonder if she's having a little joke?

Chapter Twenty-Three
Year Three – Family Matters

LAVANDE'S current guests are a gentle couple from Scotland. They tell me they have a severely mentally and physically disabled son of 15, who needs care 24 hours a day. They have managed to get him into a care home for a week so that they can have a rest, as they are both permanently exhausted. Friends and family members clubbed together to pay for their flight and holiday – the first they have had in 15 years. Being able to lie in bed in the morning, to be able to sit and read and to have a meal together without one of them having to feed their child, they say, has made them feel reborn. Friends and family are also visiting the boy daily, and phone to report that he is happy and being well cared for. After the first few days, though, they admit that they are missing their child and longing to be back home with him. I bless my good fortune in having two healthy children, something I'd always taken for granted, and wonder how I would have coped if things had turned out otherwise.

A new family arrives, with four young children who are as attractive as they are polite. They say "please" and "thank you," and are confident without being cocky. The eldest, fifteen-year-old Tim is followed by Charlie, 14, Sally, 12, and enchanting, fairy-like Mahalia who is very-nearly-almost-four - "an afterthought," and the planet around which the rest of the family happily orbit. Their parents devote each day to entertaining and amusing the children, and have been and bought them an inflatable swimming pool. They go on cycle rides through the fields, collecting wild flowers and interesting stones. They draw, write and read their stories aloud and play charades. The children have built a make-shift tent in the garden with a tarpaulin, and they are always happy, and always kind and polite to each other. If somebody set out to create the perfect family, this is how it would be. I have given them the freedom of our garden and paddock, as all the children are animal-mad and will happily spend hours brushing the cats and dogs, watching the pond activity, and feeding the horses apples and carrots. Mahalia also gives them cornflakes from her tiny, sticky hands, and both horses lick her gently. The dogs are always licking her, too, because her face and clothes are generally smothered with chocolate, jam or ice cream.

Margaret, their mother, says that the highlight of their day is the hunt for eggs laid by our hens. I have told them that any they find are theirs – we have plenty. Our birds are a strange mob, some roost in the trees, some in the barn, and some disappear completely at night but are always waiting for their morning feed. They lay their eggs in the oddest places, but seldom in the designated nest boxes, and the four children are up and out early each morning in the hope of discovering a cache. They search among the bales of straw and hay, the flowerbeds, the boles of trees, and from the house I hear their occasional shouts of triumph. None of them actually like eating eggs, says Margaret, but they just love finding them. Margaret makes a lot of cakes, meringues and custards during their two-week stay. "Holiday treats," she explains. "We are 'healthy eaters' but for two weeks of the year we indulge ourselves."

By the time they have been here a couple of days they feel like family, and the kids are in and out of the house, borrowing books or offering to help. They enjoy sweeping floors and washing dishes, which they do very thoroughly, and have a passion for tidying kitchen drawers. Never have the drawers been tidier, and never have I had such difficulty in finding things after one of their zealous reorganisations.

Mahalia has commanded a picnic, and the whole family are busy preparing for it. I am invited, and it's just wonderful. We take it down to the end of the field, beneath a huge oak tree, and spread out a blanket on the ground. Margaret has made sandwiches and little sausages on sticks, and there are rice crispy cakes, an angel cake (that used up a dozen egg whites!) and cubes of jelly, and I have contributed elderflower cordial and ice-cream. We have races and play hide-and-seek, which is a challenge as there is only the oak tree to hide behind and nobody is allowed to find Mahalia. Mark, their father, takes photographs and fends off wasps and Mahalia gently collects up the streams of ants that are over-running the food and carries them ten yards away. She patiently continues to do this for at least half an hour, earnestly concerned with not injuring them. She is now covered in ants, but resists any suggestion that she needs a shower to flush them off. "Mustn't hurt them," she says. Then we think up a good game - chasing each other with the hose. As the temperature is in the high 30s we are all enthusiastic about the idea, and are soon drenched. Mahalia is ant-free and has forgotten about them.

My mare Leila has been retired for many years, and has a gentle nature although she is a rather large and lively animal with a reputation for having a mind of her own and no brakes. So one morning when I look out I am horrified to see her jogging up the field with a very small figure bouncing up and down on her back. Running behind is Mark, and standing with her hands clamped to her mouth is Margaret. I rush down to the gate and arrive there at the same time as the horse and her passenger. Mahalia is pink-faced and clapping her hands.

"What happened?" I ask.

"Mahalia wanted to sit on her back. I thought it would be OK. I lifted her up, and the horse just started jogging off. Mahalia was holding on to her mane and sort of slipping and sliding from one side to the other, but somehow she stayed on. I was afraid to run too fast in case it made the horse go faster. She was so gentle, almost floating. And this is amazing - just before she reached that tree, with the low branch," he points to a lime tree, "she slowed down, moved to one side, and then began jogging again. If she hadn't swerved, Mahalia would have been scraped off. That horse knew exactly what it was doing. I swear she was looking after Mahalia and just wanted to give her a bit of fun."

I put a head collar on, and recommend that Mark attaches a rope before he hoists her on board again. Mahalia is hooked. If she could, she'd be sitting on the horse all day. Although she only reaches the horses' knees, she is totally confident around them, and whenever she's out of sight, we know that she's down at the stables.

It's going to seem very quiet here, as the family are leaving tomorrow. I am really sorry to see them go, but delighted that they have already booked to return next year, with Margaret's parents, who will stay in Pissenlit. Mahalia has kissed every animal, including all the hens that we could catch, and she has feathers, leaves and some hair from the horses' tails to take home as souvenirs. We all hug and kiss and shed a few tears, and the children each give me a drawing entitled: "What I liked most about my holiday." Tim's drawing shows a teenage boy much like himself, stretched out on a sun lounger. Charlie is pictured eating a whole baguette, and Sally has drawn a picture of the cats. Predictably, Mahalia's drawing is a collage of strange creatures – hens with four legs, horses that look like dachshunds, and blobs with limbs sticking out at strange angles. She is going to send an apple and carrot every day, she promises. And she is also going to tell her special friend Baby Jeeziz to take care of all the animals.

Chapter Twenty-Four
Year Three – The Worst Time

I'VE started sorting through the things people leave behind before Ivy gets here to clean, and taking some for myself. I don't begrudge her a few bits and pieces – particularly the jam and pepper, but when she helps herself to all the alcohol, unopened foods and all the books and magazines without asking, I think it's rather greedy. I find myself rushing to get in as soon as guests have left so that I too get a chance for some goodies. Then I feel mean.

When she arrives today, she's in a very bad mood and bangs the bucket and broom around noisily, bumping the vacuum cleaner into the furniture.

"Is anything wrong?" I ask, because from her behaviour there obviously is, and equally obviously she wants to talk about it.

"I'm furious. Absolutely furious. I feel like slashing her car tyres." She flops down into a chair on the patio with a thump.

I guess that she's referring to Fliss, who had moved out of Pissenlit at the end of March, but who has kept in touch and often pops in for a chat. Fliss had had endless trouble with tradesmen, whom she says are all incompetent and dishonest, and has already put her new house up for sale. She's thinking of buying something nearer the coast. However, the last time I saw her she was excited as Ivy had invited her to dinner to meet a potential mate. "I've just got a feeling," she said, "this is going to be Mr Right."

Ivy's rage is about broccoli and cherry tomatoes.

"I took ENORMOUS trouble to cook for the wretched woman. You know how princessy she is about food. She ate almost nothing – picked at the chicken breast – organic you know, cost a ransom, far more than I could afford – wouldn't touch the cherry tomatoes, and only took the tips off the broccoli – wasted all the stems. So rude. I was brought up to eat what I was offered when I was invited out. Manners maketh man."

"Oh dear," I say. "It was rude."

"I shan't ask her again. Anyway, I've run out of men. Alan wasn't interested. 'No F-factor,' he said, and something rather masculine about her. And she's too fussy: this one's too old; that one's too creepy; that one can't get it up, that one's too mean. For God's sake, I've done my best, but I can't work miracles."

Fliss is very indiscreet about her liaisons, and discusses the shortcomings of the various men in intimate detail. My English reserve makes me very uncomfortable listening to her descriptions of their peculiar personal habits and sexual prowess – or lack of – but she has no qualms and seems to need to pour out her heart to somebody, and as she has no family here or close friends, I seem to be the only candidate.

I make soothing noises because Ivy's getting very red in the face and looks as if she might have a heart attack. Then I'll be back to doing the cleaning myself.

"Well, never mind, you've tried your best. Perhaps it's better to just leave her to find her own man."

"If indeed that's what she actually wants," says Ivy in a lowered tone. "I think Alan may be right. She can be very aggressive, and I don't believe she's quite the airhead she pretends to be. I'm pretty certain she dances at the other end of the ballroom but won't admit it." She sniffs.

In truth the thought has crossed my mind a few times, but I like Fliss. Her personal life isn't my business and I'm not going to discuss it with Ivy.

"Perhaps you could help her with her dress sense," I suggest. "She doesn't have much idea. Whereas you are always so… stylish."

Fliss has recently abandoned the mini skirts in favour of some heavy men's jeans. They don't fit at all well, and display the full division of her buttocks when she bends over. Somebody complained in a local restaurant that it was putting him off his food. I've tried to think of a way of mentioning it to her, but have been unable to find a diplomatic way to do so. And I can't help thinking she must be aware.

"Pff. Fat chance. Don't tell me she doesn't know that when she bends over she's showing six inches of bum crack. Gross. I can't make a silk purse out of a sow's ear, can I? And she's obviously on the change – all those mood swings and flushes. But I must give her a call tonight before she goes off to England. I'm out of Golden Syrup and baps."

Just after 2.00 pm a taxi pulls up, and out clambers a large ungainly woman carrying just a couple of plastic shopping bags. She's arrived two hours before the agreed booking-in time, but luckily Ivy has already left, and Pissenlit is ready. I open the gate and lead the new guest, who ignores my outstretched hand, to the cottage. She kicks out at one of our cats, who is walking beside me.

"Shoo!" she bellows at the astonished animal, which is used to being spoilt and fussed over by guests. I ask if she doesn't have any luggage, and she replies that she has all she needs for her stay, which is to give her a chance to "express her creativity."

Does she have plenty of food, I ask, mentioning that the nearest shops are nearly six miles away and there's no public transport.

"Do you not go into town yourself?" she asks. I can't identify her accent, it's guttural with sharp corners. I say I'll be happy to take her shopping with me tomorrow. By then I expect she'll be in a better mood.

She opens the door with a scowl when I knock this morning. Pointedly ignoring the open front passenger door of my car, she climbs into the back and buries her face in a magazine. We drive in complete silence to the shops, and all the way home.

I say, "I'll be going shopping again on Thursday, at mid-day if you'd like to come along."

Then she makes me jump, by shouting "Do you think it's right to keep all these damned animals when people are coming here on holiday? Don't you know they're full of diseases?"

Before I can reply she takes her shopping and slams back into Pissenlit.

Last year we had some unpleasantness with one of our guests. A Dutchman came with his English wife and a small baby. I'd had great difficulty getting a deposit from them and only when I said I'd cancel the booking unless I received it within eight days did a cheque arrive.

When they turned up, he was extremely frosty, and his wife seemed embarrassed and uncomfortable. For the week they were here he sat in the garden reading, pointedly putting down his book every time he saw me going past to the field and staring rudely, and muttering to himself. I was upset and surprised, as we have several Dutch friends, and all the other Dutch people I have ever met have always been friendly. On the day they were due to check out, there was no sign of them leaving by the agreed time of 10.00am. I left them for an hour then went and knocked on the door. There was no answer. Maybe they were having problems with the baby. When mid-day came there was still no sign of them, and Ivy had finished cleaning Pissenlit and was roaming around my house opening drawers and cupboards. I knocked hard on the door and he opened it with a glare. I said they had overstayed by two hours and that they need to leave so that we can get the cottage ready for the new guests, but he replied that they were having lunch and would leave when they had finished. Then he slammed the door in my face.

I sent Ivy home. On top of my growing anger, I didn't want to hear any more about the young girl who had thrown herself from the 4th floor of a multi-storey car park. By 2.15pm I'd worked myself into a frightful rage. I hammered on the door and said they were to leave instantly. I got out the vacuum cleaner and started shoving it around. They gathered up their baby and bags, and stowed them in their car, and then he returned and banged on the table to attract my attention.

He harangued me about lack of privacy, lack of trust, rudeness, and swindling them out of an afternoon, as they had not planned to leave until 4.00 pm. He was a big man and I was beginning to think that he was not quite right in the head. He shouted louder and his face got redder, and throbbing veins stuck out on his temples. I felt really intimidated, and started edging towards the back door, ready to stick my head out and scream if he came any closer. Then his wife came in and pulled him to their car. They drove off with a screech of tyres. When I found a pile of peanuts under the cushion of an armchair I thought it was an accident. Then I found more. Not just one or two peanuts, but hundreds. A pile beneath each mattress, a pile under all the cushions on the armchairs and settees in the living room! Eleven empty packets in the bin. Was it some bizarre message? An evil spell? Certainly very odd, and until now the only really nasty guest we have had.

I'm shocked to find that I dislike the new arrival so intensely I feel I want to go and punch her in the face. Her aggressive attitude and behaviour and the fact that she is a big, hefty woman is making me feel nervous, so I am glad that there are people staying in Lavande.

I sit for a long while, trying to think if I could have done something to make her so angry, because I'm sure it must be my fault. Surely nobody would behave like that unless they'd been offended. I dig out her booking form, and the accompanying letter, which has a web address on it. She describes herself as a contemporary artist, so I go to her website. The paintings there will give me nightmares for weeks.

Disembowelled bodies, decapitated animals, women with mutilated genitals and breasts; decaying corpses. It's a mess of red, black and purple, and it's so horrible that I wonder if she is completely mad. I also realise with relief that I'm not the cause of her behaviour.

For the week she is here the only sounds I hear are of her shouting at birds in the garden, and throwing stones at the cats, who very soon learn to keep out of range. When I get ready to go shopping on Thursday there is no sign of her. I toot the horn a couple of times, but the door remains closed.

Early on Saturday morning, a taxi arrives. She climbs in and I watch the vehicle disappear down the lane.

She's left the door of Pissenlit open, and I can hear water running. When I step into the cottage, I'm stunned. It looks as if the only thing that hasn't been vandalised is the welcome pack I had left, which is in the middle of the kitchen floor, untouched. I run up the stairs to the bathroom. The plug is in, and both taps have been turned on full. The water is half-way to the top. I pull the plug and turn off the taps. Then I go from room to room, my heart racing.

In the bedroom the curtains are hanging down from their rails, the carpet kicked into the corner, red wine staining the bed linen and mattress. Two light switches have been levered off the wall exposing the wires.

A bottle of cooking oil is tipped on its side with the lid off, and there is oil all over the kitchen surface and running down into the drawers and over the floor. The kitchen is filled with greasy crockery and cutlery, and food left-overs. Tins and cartons are scattered on the floor. The futon is covered with grease stains. A table lamp is smashed, books taken from the shelves and thrown on the floor, a pair of wooden salad servers broken in half. On the bedroom walls are graphically violent charcoal

187

sketches. Even the pillow cases have charcoal smears all over them. And it will be a fortnight before, following remarks from guests about smells and bluebottles, I trace the source to a piece of raw meat wedged behind a pipe under the sink.

My first thought is that at all costs I must stop Ivy arriving and seeing this mess. She's difficult enough when the place is clean. In a crisis she's the last person I need, so I phone and make up a story and promise to post her cheque to her.

The odd thing is that as I gape at the devastation, aside from the panic at wondering how I can possibly get the place habitable in time for the next guests, my other emotion is pity for a soul so screwed up that it can expend energy on wrecking a place for no good reason. I cannot imagine what is going on in this lunatic's head.

And I also cannot begin to think how or where to start clearing up the mess.

I need help, so I phone Tristram and Beverly. We've become good friends over the last couple of years. I've bought various bits and pieces from Tristram, and he's always happy to lend a hand when I need one. He and Beverly keep themselves to themselves and have a fairly small social circle, of which I feel privileged to be a part.

I yell at the answering machine: "Help."

This is one of those rare occasions I feel the need for alcohol, and I knock back a couple of vodka tonics and go to make a start trying to sort out the mess. Tristram arrives alone an hour and a half later, and looks at the shambles. He runs his fingers through his hair and says, uncharacteristically "Shit - this is bad. Whoever did this is insane."

It's the first time I've ever heard him swear. He's derisive of anybody who can't express their emotions without cursing.

"Let's do it," he says, and armed with bin bags, buckets of hot water, kitchen roll, and an array of cleaning products, we begin to clear up. We work frantically, soaking up the grease from the kitchen, washing out the inside of units, mopping at the stained mattress then drying it with a hair drier. Tristram has the answer for the futon: sprinkle it with cornflour, allow it to soak up the grease, then vacuum it. It takes out some, but not all, and there are still visible marks.

"You'll need to get the covers cleaned later. For now we'll put some throws over."

Our efforts to get the sketches off the walls result in grey smudges, and we slap a thick coat of emulsion over them. It should just about be dry when the next guests arrive. They still show through faintly, but it's the best we can do. We spray the rooms, open the windows wide and put on electric fans to get the paint smell out.

"Did you take a deposit against damages from this person?"

I shake my head. "We normally accept people on trust."

"Then in future I think you should. This is wanton destruction."

When we've done as much as we can we sit over the habitual mint tea. I notice that Tristram is looking tired and miserable.

"How are the children?" I ask.

"Oh, they're just wonderful. Just wonderful."

"And how's Beverly? What's he up to?"

"Beverly has gone."

"Gone where?"

"Just gone. Away. Somewhere. Anywhere. I don't know. Gone for good."

"What! What do you mean, he's gone for good?"

"Just that. He's left. Disappeared."

"Do you want to talk about it?"

"We've been together for 18 years. We've never had a row. Hardly spent a day apart. We were so happy. At least I thought so."

"I thought so too. You seemed such a perfect match. When did he go?"

"Six days ago. I drove some stuff up to Paris, to a dealer there. When I got back in the evening, he'd gone. Cleared out all his clothes, books, pictures. It's as if he was never there."

"But didn't he leave a note? Phone? Hasn't he contacted you?"

"Nothing. I've phoned all our friends, and no-one's heard from him. Or they're not telling me," he says darkly.

"Maybe he's had some sort of emotional crisis. I'm sure he'll come back."

"No," said Tristram quietly, "he won't come back. I know it in my soul. I can feel an empty space. I've gone over and over it in my mind, and there's no answer, other than Beverly wanted to go, for reasons of his own. But I wish he'd at least said goodbye." His voice is thick.

"What are you going to do?"

"I don't know yet. I can't really think straight. I feel as if I'm in a dream or a play. Nothing feels real."

Cautiously, I put an arm around his shoulder. He takes my hand and squeezes it to his chest.

"Is there any way at all that I can help? Anything at all? If you want to go away for a while, I could have the children here." His Dachsies get on perfectly well with our dogs.

"No, thank you for offering. But they need me, and I need them even more. And I need time to think. At the moment I want to be alone."

"Then come over whenever you like. I won't contact you, but please, keep in touch. Bring the children. Phone any time, day or night."

"I will. Don't worry. I'll be OK."

But as he walks to his car he looks smaller, less golden, suddenly greyer and older.

This hasn't been a good week.

Chapter Twenty-Five
Year Three – Dolly's Miracle

ON Saturday afternoons I always shut the dogs away until new arrivals have settled, so that they are not overwhelmed by joyful canine greetings. Today, however, blind Dolly has found her way out of the garden, and is standing at the gate wagging her tail expectantly. Everybody loves Dolly. Or has done until now. A tall and very thin woman stands the other side of the gate, rigid with fear.

"On no," she breathes, "not a dog."

A bearded man stretches out his hand.

"Martin. I'm afraid Barbara is very frightened of dogs."

Only when Dolly is locked in the house does Barbara step cautiously through the gate. She's embarrassed and apologetic.

"It can't get in here, can it?" she asks.

I assure her that Dolly is and will remain safely contained in our garden behind a strong fence, and add that even in the very unlikely event that they did find themselves face to face, the most that Dolly would do would be to lick her to death. She is the most gentle and loving dog imaginable. Barbara clutches her throat, with an expression that indicates that if she should find herself face to face with Dolly, she will go into immediate cardiac arrest.

She has no idea why she has this fear of dogs, which she acknowledges is irrational. She has never been bitten or chased. She won't go onto a beach, or into a park for fear of a dog coming near her. Her mother was the same.

"I wonder," I said, "if that's where your fear comes from? I'm claustrophobic, and was told that my mother was too, although she left when I was very small and I hardly knew her. So I absolutely understand your feelings."

It's quite likely, she agrees. She doesn't dislike dogs; she's just afraid of them. It's a dreadful inconvenience, and an embarrassment. They have several friends with dogs and visits to them are always traumatic. She has tried hypnotism, without success. I give her my word that Dolly will not come near her. She is safe behind the fence. I add that we have five more dogs – her eyes widen - and that they are equally friendly and equally well contained.

Dolly is perplexed as these are the first guests (apart from the crazed woman) who have not wanted to play with or make a fuss of her. She's become used to being the centre of attention. She stands with her nose poking through the trellis, wagging her tail slowly in a hopeful manner. After a couple of days Barbara is satisfied that the dogs cannot get near her, and relaxes sufficiently to stand a couple of yards away, and even tosses them scraps from the barbecue. Dolly has only two thoughts in her gentle, sightless head: food and cuddles. We had found her abandoned and starving. A few months of love and good food restored her health, but then she developed diabetes and eventually became blind. Her blindness seems to cause her no problems as she has learnt her way around the house and garden and knows how to avoid obstacles.

At the first whiff of smoke Dolly stands on her hind legs, front paws hooked through the trellis, her blind eyes pointing at the barbecue. Barbara remarks that she has the gentlest eyes and sweetest expression she has ever seen, and wonders how anybody could have been cruel enough to abandon her.

Martin signals me over to the fence one morning.

"You won't believe this, but B. actually touched Dolly's head this morning! I'm really amazed. I never thought it would happen."

Barbara is astonished at herself, and tells me that she is 41 and has never voluntarily touched a dog in her life, but now she feels she is "bonding" with Dolly, whom she is even allowing to lick pieces of sausage from her fingers.

At the beginning of their second week, I take some eggs round to the cottage one afternoon, and Martin puts his fingers to his lips, and whispers

"Come and look."

Barbara is sitting on the settee. Next to her, Dolly is stretched out with her head on Barbara's thigh. She raises one ear briefly, gives a small sigh and goes back to sleep. Barbara smiles radiantly, and apologises for letting the dog on the furniture.

"I hope you don't mind, but she scratched at the gate and asked to come in, and she looked so pitiful that I couldn't refuse. Then she lolloped straight through the door and hopped up here. She's so gentle."

By the end of the fortnight Dolly has almost left home and taken up residence in Lavande. Barbara brushes her, feeds her and spoils her with titbits, and wishes from the bottom of her heart she could take Dolly back to Scotland with her. When they leave, she kisses Dolly on her black nose, strokes her ears once, and bursts into tears. Martin's eyes are moist, and I have a lump in my throat.

"You have no idea," says Barbara, "what Dolly has done for me. I love her to bits. If you'd told me that I'd ever fall in love with a dog, I'd have said you were mad. But it has really happened. I'm going to miss her so much. If only we could take her with us."

As they drive away Barbara's face is a mixture of grief and joy. Dolly, listening to the fading engine noise, has no idea of the miracle she has wrought. She's waiting hopefully at the gate for our next visitors.

Chapter Twenty-Six
Year Three – Darling, Look, a Tiny Little Hip Bath!

SUCH sad news today. Annie, the American lady whose family are coming to stay next year, emails to say that Brad is dead. He had been suffering from cancer for a couple of years, and knew that his last visit to France would indeed be his last visit.

"He was a strange little guy," she wrote, "but we were very fond of him. And he never stopped talking about how much he enjoyed meeting you and staying at your home. He said it was one of his best trips to France."

I hope that's true. As Annie says, he was an oddball but a gentle soul, and our friendship had given me a great deal of pleasure.

Some years December can be a beautiful month of mild, bright days, with clear skies. Crisp mornings when you can sit outside in a jumper, to sip your morning coffee. Fresh, clear days perfect for walking, and chilly evenings warmed by a wood fire and 20-tog duvet. This year is one of those. The early morning chill flushes your lungs, and the aroma of woodsmoke from neighbouring chimneys fills the air. It's glorious, and even more so when a late booking comes in for Pissenlit for ten days over Christmas and New Year.

Tanya and George have written to say that they love what they have seen on our website, and are looking forward to a cosy and romantic stay in the little cottage, their first Christmas as man and wife. They arrive in a sleek people carrier from which they unload several matching suitcases, two cases of wine, a great big wicker hamper and a cool box. Tanya is incredibly beautiful and sickeningly slim, wearing high-heeled boots and a fur coat with many panels that swing as she strides towards the gate. She holds out a delicate tanned hand sporting a two-carat solitaire diamond, and smiles to show her perfect white teeth. I am back-footed already, and that is before George bounds over, tall, lithe, and equally tanned and beautifully-toothed and dressed. I have a horrible feeling in the pit of my stomach. These glamorous people are in the wrong place.

"Hi," tinkles Tanya. "How lovely to meet you! Such a glorious drive down. How long have you been here? How did you find it? Aren't the roof tiles gorgeous! It's all so quaint! The countryside is fantastic! George says we should buy a holiday home here."

I stand slack-mouthed as a mantle of doom and foreboding descends around me. I would like to keep them standing here chatting in happy anticipation for the next ten days, but taking a deep breath and one of the wine cases, I lead them to Pissenlit. I push open the door, and usher them in. I've lit the fire earlier, so the room is warm and welcoming, and so not what they are expecting.

"Oh," says Tanya in dismay. "I thought it was an open fire. So we could see the flames." We all stare accusingly at the cast iron stove. I point out the pile of logs, and the metal hook for removing the lid of the stove to replenish it.

"Good Lord," says George.

"It's a bit smaller than I thought," he says. "Tiny, in fact." He rubs his head ruefully, having already banged it on the low beam over the door.

Smiling weakly, I take them up the stairs to the bedroom, which is spacious and meets with their approval. Tanya feels the mattress. "Oh good, nice and firm. And I love the throw." She strokes the heavy faux-fur cover over the thick duvet.

"Here's your bathroom," I say, and we all try and crowd into the teeny space. George backs out, Tanya squeezes herself beside the lavatory, and I push the door closed so she can see the bath with shower over.

"I've always wanted to try a hip bath," says Tanya gamely, while for the first time I try to imagine what it will be like to sit in a short, shallow bath on a cold winter's day. She slides out of the bathroom.

"George, darling, look, a tiny little hip bath."

George puts his head round the door and says "Ah."

"Well, never mind, I'm sure we'll be absolutely fine. Let's get ourselves unpacked." Tanya turns around in a circle looking for somewhere to put the hamper and the wine cases, while George lugs the suitcases up the stairs. I show them the CD player, and the board games and books, and assure them that anything I can do to make their stay the fairytale they have been looking forward to, I will do with the greatest enthusiasm.

Five minutes later George taps at the front door. He has a frozen turkey clutched to his chest.

"It won't fit in the freezer," he says apologetically. "I wonder if you have room for it in yours? It's organic."

"Of course, no problem," I lie.

We have a medium-sized fridge-freezer. The freezer section is designed to hold a few bags of frozen vegetables and some ice-creams. George and Tanya's turkey is not particularly large, as turkeys go, but still to fit it in I have to remove both drawers, push it with my foot, and quickly slam the door. I phone a friend and borrow some freezer space for our displaced vegetables.

At 6.30 pm George and Tanya knock on the door to say they are going out for dinner, and ask which of our local restaurants I recommend. There is a choice of two. The good one is only open in the evenings from Thursdays to Sundays - today is Tuesday - and the bad one isn't open at all in the evenings. The next nearest, where the food is spectacular is open, but fully booked, and I finally find them a table at a reasonable place nine miles away. I have to give them full marks for courtesy. Although it is already crystal clear that they have made a terrible mistake in booking Pissenlit, they are clearly taking pains not to offend or embarrass me.

Vaguely I wonder what they had expected for £130 ($170) for a ten-day stay, and whether they had properly looked at the photographs and read the descriptions on our website. They really should have been in a spacious log cabin in the Alps, with a jacuzzi, crackling logs and views over snowy mountains.

Next day I'm having lunch when the dogs start barking at the back door. I go towards the window and see, tiptoeing down the drive, George with two suitcases, followed by Tanya with a case of wine. They load these into the boot of their car, and come back, still tiptoeing, for a second run.

I debate for a few seconds what to do, and decide that if they have chosen to leave like that, I should allow them to do so without embarrassing them or myself. When their car has driven away, I go into Pissenlit and find a note on the table. It reads:

"Dear Suzy,

We have just had dreadful news. Tanya's father has had a heart attack, and we have to return to London immediately. We did not want to disturb you. Thank you for your very warm welcome and all your help, and forgive our hasty departure. We will get in touch once we are back home. With love from Tanya and George."

They have left a bottle of Chablis Grand Cru with a Merry Christmas tag tied around the neck.

We never hear from Tanya and George again, although I half-expect a polite letter requesting a refund. I only hope that in exchange for their disappointment, they managed to amuse their friends with the tale of their terrible Christmas. They haven't been our most satisfied guests, but they are certainly the most gracious.

Now – what shall we do with the turkey?

Nudists by Elle Ford

Chapter Twenty-Seven
Year Four – Friendship

THIS is going to turn out to be a strange year, not only because I'm going to be living in a tent for two months, but because of what happens in February.

Last year a couple staying in Pissenlit wanted me to pray with them. They were evangelists for something called The Church of Sweet Running Waters, and more persistent than even the Jehovah's Witnesses who call regularly and hand me their magazine (in French) through the gate. The couple, Lynn and Art had tambourines that they tinkled at 8.30 each morning, while they sang hymns in the garden.

"Come and join us!" they called, beatific smiles pointed my way.

Although I explained that I am not religious, but respect the views of all religions, they were not deterred, and kept pressing pamphlets upon me and telling me that Jesus loved and would save me. They were delightful, fun people when they weren't talking religion.

Since they left they've kept in touch with postcards and emails, and at Christmas sent a card with a brochure about their church. Then yesterday I had an email from Lynn asking if she can phone me regarding a private and sensitive matter on Tuesday evening, when Art will be out.

When she rings I couldn't be more surprised at her request.

"I know you're a very kind and Christian lady," she starts.

"I am not," I reply, emphatically, anticipating some need that I'll be unable to fulfil.

"Yes you are. You're the only person I can think of who could help somebody in a dreadful situation."

I wait.

"It's about a baby."

I imagine a baby arriving on my doorstep in a basket.

"What is wrong with the baby ?" I asked. "I couldn't possibly have it here."

"It's against everything I believe in, and I know you'll be shocked, but..."

She's crying, and I interrupt.

"Are you talking about an abortion?"

She sobs.

I don't have strong personal feelings regarding abortion. Other people's lives are not my concern, but I am bewildered as to how I am to be involved. When Lynn can talk, a story emerges of a terrible incident, somebody who is pregnant who shouldn't be, and how a family will be destroyed unless the pregnancy can be terminated, and how Lynn has to put aside her personal feelings in the interest of the family.

It's all very confusing and esoteric and I don't want to know the details, but what it comes down to is that Lynn wants me to make the arrangements for a termination in France, and she and the lady concerned will come out here on a supposedly girlie break, staying for a week until the deed has been accomplished. Money isn't a problem.

Since we started our holiday homes my life has quite often taken on a surreal quality. I'm used to dealing with unusual situations but this one is in a different league entirely.

I go and talk to a local doctor who is known to be sympathetic to embarrassing pregnancies, and who will make the necessary arrangements. However, he will need to see the patient beforehand.

Dates are arranged and Lynn organises the travel arrangements for herself and her friend. She is in a state of terrible distress not only because of what she believes to be the crime of abortion, but equally the fact that she is deceiving Art. When she and Bella arrive by car Bella is withdrawn and pale but composed. Lynn is determinedly positive. They are sharing Pissenlit, and decline an invitation to have a meal with me tonight.

Once I've taken Bella to see the doctor, who is satisfied that all is as it should be, we drive the following morning to the private clinic. She's admitted at 3.00pm, and we are told to collect her the following afternoon. Bella speaks no French and looks bewildered but resigned, and the nurses are gentle with her as they settle her into a small room.

Once we have left the clinic Lynn explodes into a torrent of tears, and asks God to forgive her. She's really in quite a frightful state of anxiety and guilt. Between the clinic and our home is a Benedictine monastery with a rather lovely chapel where the monks hold their daily church services. It's very plain and simple; there are no images or icons, only a small brass crucifix on a raised area at one end, and a floral display next to it. It's somewhere that I always find very peaceful and beautiful, despite my lack of religious beliefs. The chapel is relatively modern, and features abstract stained glass windows all around. As the sun makes its daily journey from east to west, it strikes the windows, casting pools of trembling pastel shades upon the creamy walls and floor. These follow the sun's orbit, creating a slow-moving film of gentle light. It's somewhere I go just to enjoy the peace and simplistic beauty.

I drive Lynn there and suggest we go and sit quietly for a while. She sits for what seems like hours, eyes closed, clutching my hand and making little moaning noises. Then she turns to me, smiles and says "His will be done," and stands up.

It's a cold and miserable early spring day, and when we get home we swaddle ourselves in warm clothes and take the dogs for a long, long walk.

She wants to explain about Bella, but I would rather not know. It isn't my business. That evening she insists on taking me out for a meal, and chats about her life in England and her job as a social worker. By tacit agreement we do not discuss religion. She phones Art when we get home, tells him about the chapel, the walk, the meal, with no mention of the clinic.

Then we play Scrabble until long after midnight, and drink a little more wine than we should.

The clinic telephone next morning to say that Bella is fine and we can collect her any time.

When she appears with her small overnight bag, Lynn opens her arms silently and folds Bella into them. I think what a great act of friendship this is, when one can put another's needs before one's own at the cost of so much private grief. It's a powerful example of altruism.

I don't see anything of them before they leave two days later, when they knock on the door and shake hands. In Pissenlit there is an envelope propped up on the kitchen table. Inside is a card with a photograph of a stained glass window. It says: "God bless." There is also €600 ($770) in cash. That is the last I ever hear from Lynn.

Chapter Twenty-Eight
Year Four – Teenagers

THERE are four females staying in Lavande this week – two mothers with their two teenage girls. I'm a little concerned as to how they will entertain the girls as we are far from any major shopping centre or nightlife. Both women are single parents – Marian is something senior in the National Health Service, and Helen is a teacher. They say their jobs are extremely stressful and they are desperate to just chill out, soak up the sun, read a few books and crack a few bottles. I have mentioned that there isn't a lot for youngsters to do, but both mothers seem confident that the girls will enjoy the sun and the animals.

From their expressions when they arrive, I think it unlikely. Ticia, as she likes to be called, has the body, the looks, the hair, the money and the attitude. Lesley is quieter and looks more studious. She has braces on her teeth and hasn't yet developed Ticia's poise or shape. Both look uncomfortable, out of place, and not at all ecstatic to be here.

"Jeez," says Ticia loudly, "welcome to Crapsville." Lesley laughs nervously, at the same time glancing apologetically at me, aware that I've heard Ticia. Ticia tells her mother, Marian, to get her sun screen as she's going to lie in the garden, just in case there's a decent sun lounger, although she doubts it. Marian digs out a tube and asks Ticia if she's going to change into her bikini. "No, mother dear, I am not wearing a bikini until I get a new one." She snatches the sun cream rudely and clacks out onto the patio in her high heels. The two mothers stand smiling ruefully. "Teenagers, who'd have them?"

asks Marian. Not me, I think, as I show them around the cottage.

With Ticia relaxing, the other three go about sorting out their luggage. Lesley heaves her suitcase and Ticia's up to the bedroom, while the women load the fridge with provisions they've bought on the way.

A blood-curdling, terrifying, shriek nearly stops my heart. Helen, Lesley's mother, drops her bags and leaps up the stairs, with Marian and myself close behind. Lesley is standing in the corridor, screaming and shaking, jumping from one leg to the other.

"Darling!" Helen rushes to her, "whatever has happened?"

"Spider," sobs Lesley. "A huge spider." She starts screaming again. While Helen gently ushers Lesley down the stairs, I go with Marian to fight the spider. I'm terrified of them, too, so I go and get a long-handled brush and a mug to capture it with.

We can't find it. It isn't on the walls, the window or the ceiling. Marian calls down to the still-sobbing Lesley, to ask her where she saw it, and in between sobs she says it was on the window frame. We look closely, but all we can find is one of the tiny, ethereal harvesters, which even I can pick up in my hand.

"Is this it?" I ask, from the doorway. Lesley screams and screams and runs to stand behind the sofa. It's going to be a very long week, I fear. The whole place is a harvester's dream. They live in every corner, on every beam, behind every piece of furniture, on every shelf.

The two women quickly settle down with their books and glasses of wine, but from the garden I can hear Ticia complaining that she's bored. "Darling, we've only just arrived!"

"Well, I'm ready to go home. What a dump."

Next day I ask the girls if they'd like to come and see our horses. Lesley would, as long as they are out in the field, and not the barn where there will be spiders. Ticia says no thank you, she rides in Hyde Park and seeing horses just standing around isn't her thing.

Lesley would like to go to the local swimming pool, but Ticia wouldn't unless she can go to town to buy a new costume. The ladies don't want to drive up there after having spent most of the previous day travelling, so Ticia snorts and slams a door. Perhaps the girls would enjoy a couple of hours at a nearby park, which has tennis courts, mini-golf and a large lake for swimming, I suggest. Ticia turns up her nose at the idea, but Lesley is enthusiastic so I say I'll go with her, at which point Ticia changes her mind and decides she'll come too. After she has packed a large shoulder bag with everything she'll need, I drive them there and say I'll be back in a couple of hours.

The mothers are grateful and mellow, sitting in the garden reading and sipping wine. When I return to collect the girls and ask if they enjoyed themselves, Lesley says it was great, and Ticia flings her arms about and shouts: "Oh yes, it was really wild! We met a load of boys with motorbikes, and they're taking us up to town to a disco tonight. I'm SO pleased to be here!"

"Really?" I say, proud to have elicited something positive from Ticia, but alarmed at what the mothers will say about their daughters going off on motorbikes with strange boys.

"No, not really." Ticia's sarcastic voice brings me back to earth. "As if. But thanks very much for bringing us here. Now can we go back, please?"

It is apparent that Ticia is the kind of girl who wants what she wants, when she wants it, and if she doesn't get it she will make everybody around her just as sorry as she possibly can.

While Ticia has the looks, Lesley has the charm and is by far the more attractive of the two girls because of her intelligence, gentle nature, and desire to please everybody. Ticia wants everything her way, and makes sure she gets it - whatever it takes. Sometimes she shows brief flashes of sweetness, but she is going through the hateful teenager phase, and is hateful.

The only difficulty that Lesley presents is her terror of spiders. Before she goes to bed, everybody must search every corner of her room to make sure that it's safe, and she sleeps with a cotton sheet over her head to prevent them getting on her in the night. Whenever there is a piercing shriek we know that Lesley has spotted a spider.

World-weary and bored, Ticia doesn't make any attempt to disguise the fact. She never emerges from her room before mid-day, and when she does it is in her pyjamas. She tosses her artfully-tousled hair, stretches her arms above her head and yawns theatrically as if she has just woken, when everybody knows she's been listening to her iPod for hours and experimenting with make-up. This strategy ensures that any planned outings for the day are sabotaged right from the start, unless it is to the shopping centres, when she miraculously arises at 6.00am and has breakfast on the table for 7.00am. She flaunts her purchases, and has a foot-stamping tantrum when her mother declines to buy her a pair of trainers that cost €158

($205). She talks loudly into her mobile phone about radio interviews, modelling assignments and weekend house parties, while Lesley clutches a paper bag with a lipstick and eye-shadow and tries not to look envious.

While Ticia dreams of stardom, Lesley is firmly committed to becoming a landscape gardener. Plants are her passion, and the four of them are going for a day's outing to the magical gardens at Villandry, a couple of hours' drive away. This is the only request that Lesley has made for her personal enjoyment, and Ticia's mother is insistent that her daughter will be up and ready to leave at the same time as everybody else.

Next morning she is dressed in her unique style, made-up, demure, and has breakfast on the table for everybody. They all make a tremendous fuss of her, clear away the dishes, and are ready to leave. Unfortunately it's a bit of a drizzly morning, but it looks as if the sun will probably break through fairly soon. Lesley's mother switches on the car engine, and they all get in, except Ticia, who has disappeared. They check the bathroom, they come to my house, they look in the barns, they call out and they hoot. Ticia has vanished. At first we all hunt around casually, thinking that she is just being mischievous, but after ten minutes when we have walked round the fields and looked in every possible place, panic sets in, and in two cars we set off to search the area. I'm torn between anxiety and the faint hope that she's managed to get herself to the railway station and back to where she belongs. We soon find her lying on the grass verge beside the road, damp and defiant.

Her mother leaps out of the car and asks her whatever she thinks she is doing, but Ticia is playing deaf and dumb, and with a rude shrug stalks back to Lavande and slams the door shut. It takes half an hour of pleading with Ticia, coaxing Ticia, threatening Ticia, and finally bribing Ticia with a promise of the €158 trainers she was denied the previous day, before she climbs triumphantly into the car.

They return in the evening, and for once Lesley is glowing with excitement. She has several books and posters from Villandry, and hundreds of digital photographs. She is so animated and excited that she doesn't even bother hunting for spiders. Ticia has reverted to bored and is plugged into her iPod with her eyes closed. She's much brighter next afternoon when they return from a shopping expedition. As well as the trainers she has several silver bangles, a pair of designer jeans and a Rastafarian woolly hat. Lesley is ecstatic, and has her nose buried in a catalogue from the local garden centre and a packet of seeds. Despite the difference between the two, they are firm friends.

One day when Ticia has learnt and accepted that she is not the hub of the universe, I haven't any doubt at all that she will make herself a successful career in whatever direction she chooses. As for sweet Lesley, once her braces come off and she has developed some curves, she could well turn out to be a beauty.

When they leave, I have very mixed feelings. The two mothers and I have become good friends; they are both interesting and intelligent women and I have enjoyed their company and admired their handling of the teenagers. On their final morning the women put their foot down firmly and designate the cleaning of Lavande to the girls. Lesley sets to it willingly, while Ticia claims a bad back and a headache and sits at the bottom of the garden reading and listening to her iPod. When they leave, Lesley gives me a big hug, but true to form, Ticia keeps everybody waiting and leaves without a word.

In the afternoon, Ivy arrives sober in black, with a long string of pearls and little velvet pumps. She has brought a bin liner full of frilly lace curtains, two bundles of glossy magazines and a set of cushions for garden furniture. Also three prints of soulful children with eyes brimming with tears. One holds a bedraggled teddy-bear, another is sucking its thumb while the third is offering a bunch of flowers to an old woman. They are hideous, but she feels they will brighten up "her little empire" for incoming guests. She's turning on the charm, and so as not to spoil the ambience I bite my tongue and leave her to install her improvements. When she's gone I'll quickly whip round and take them all down, and write myself a reminder in huge letters to replace them before her next visit. This little ritual has now turned into one of those mad activities like The Generation Game as I try to outwit her. Still, it's good to keep the brain working. After I had learned of Brad's death I mentioned to her one day that I'd decided to end our relationship "for personal reasons." I couldn't bear the thought of her glee if she learned he had died. Now instead she'll be forever wondering what had happened.

Chapter Twenty-Nine
Year Four – Elvis Comes To Stay

TWO couples have taken both cottages for a fortnight. They email to say that as they will be arriving very late, I should not wait up, but just leave the keys in the doors and the outside lights on. Which is what I do.

Early next morning I'm watering the plants when rapid footsteps crunch across the hateful gravel, and a large, toned man in shorts and trainers sprints past and into the kitchen of Lavande, waving a hand as he goes. A few moments later he emerges with a basket of washing that he pins onto the line in the courtyard, and shortly afterwards he's back with a tea tray, a stack of newspapers, a heap of paperback books, a radio, an iPod, a laptop computer and two mobile phones, which he lays out neatly on the table. Plugging in his iPod earphones he sits down beneath the sunshade and begins to work his way through the newspapers.

Elvis is singing in Pissenlit. Nobody ever has, or ever will, have a voice like The King. It's deep and sensual and effortlessly powerful and it makes my toes curl. He's belting out "A Fool Such as I." It's a version I haven't heard before, with some improvisations .... la la la la la las and dum-de-dums. Outside, a slim lady with high cheekbones and very large brown eyes is setting a table. She returns my wave with a shy smile, and holds aloft the coffee jug. "Please come and have a coffee!" Her voice is gentle, friendly.

"I'm Angela," she says, pouring the coffee. "Would you like some breakfast? I'm making it now." I decline, and sit watching her going backwards and forwards to the kitchen and laying out a massive array of food - six croissants, a large slab of creamy butter, a pot of jam and jug of coffee, milk in a jug and sugar in a bowl; salt, pepper, and HP sauce. From the kitchen waft aromas of toast and bacon. Elvis, meanwhile, has moved onto "Suspicious Minds".

I ask the name of the CD, because I'd like to buy a copy.

"Oh, that's not a CD, it's my husband, George," she says.

A man appears in the doorway, one hand clutching a very small towel around his magnificent waist, the other hand over his chest, and he's singing "Love Me Tender." I have never heard anybody who can so perfectly capture the King's voice. A dribble of coffee leaks out of my open mouth and rolls down my chin.

"My goodness," I say. "What an incredible voice."

He bursts into a medley of Roy Orbison, Ricky Nelson, Buddy Holly, and he really does sound like them – not impersonators of them, but them. I am enthralled.

Angela sets down a laden tray on the table.

"Sit down and eat your breakfast, George."

George thumps down onto a chair and demolishes four sausages, six rashers of bacon, two fried eggs, four slices of toast, a heap of mushrooms and four grilled tomatoes. Then he starts on the croissants, slathering them with jam, but no butter because it makes you fat. I don't think I have ever seen man or beast with such an appetite, and I doubt Elvis could beat him in an eating contest.

Angela nibbles delicately on a croissant and sips her coffee.

After ten minutes of steady munching, George, whose modesty is clinging on with its fingertips, mops his plate with a final chunk of croissant, and rubs his Buddha-like tummy.

"That, Aunty, was very welcome. Now, when are you going shopping for our lunch?"

I mention that the only supermarket open on Sunday closes at 11.45.

"You'd better get going," he says anxiously, "otherwise we'll have nothing to eat."

Obediently she picks up the car keys, saying that she was thinking of making a pasta dish for lunch, followed by ice cream and tinned fruit, and that for dinner he might like a nice steak with chips and vegetables.

That all sounds perfect, he agrees, but don't bother with the vegetables. He'll have two steaks instead, and a couple of jacket potatoes with the chips, and not to forget to get some biscuits and cakes for tea. He rubs his tummy in anticipation. Shaking her head, smiling, Angela sets off with the map I have drawn, while George delivers Neil Diamond, Bobby Darin, Paul Anka, and more Elvis. I could sit here very happily listening to him all day, but from Lavande comes the sound of a tinkling bell.

"Oh shit, there it goes," says George.

"What do you want, Phil?" he calls.

The bell tinkles again.

"I'm not dressed. I've only just had me breakfast."

Once again the bell tinkles.

George rolls his eyes, sighs, climbs up, holding the towel strategically, and calls out

"Give me ten minutes."

"Five minutes," calls the bell-ringer.

For the next fortnight, any time I close my eyes I am transported back to the 60s, courtesy of George's powerful and beautiful voice which can be heard daily from mid-morning to just before midnight, frequently interrupted by the tinkly bell.

"Come on darlin'," George calls every time he seems me. "What yer doin' all on yer own? Get yourself over here – Auntie Angela's making scones." Or a sponge cake. Or ginger biscuits.

Auntie Angela spends 98% of her day cooking something, cheerfully, and expertly, and very necessarily, to feed George's unquenchable appetite, as a wren might try to fill a cuckoo's gaping maw. Watching him eat reminds me of Humphrey Bogart stoking the African Queen.

Over at Lavande, there is an entirely different ambience. Cooking smells rarely waft into the air, and never before 9.00pm. By the time I am up and dressed in the morning, Phil has run 10 miles, made his breakfast, cleaned the kitchen, washed their clothes and hung them on the line, vacuumed the cottage, plucked any stray weeds from the flowerbeds, and is sitting in the sun listening and reading. He says that listening simultaneously to the news on the radio and music on his iPod, while scanning the papers, sitting in the sunshine, in a peaceful garden, is his idea of paradise.

His partner Maria only begins to stir at noon, when she starts her day with half an hour of meditation followed by a further half an hour of yoga exercises. OMMMMMMMMMMMs resonate through the bedroom window. She spends another half an hour in the bathroom, and another dressing, before finally gliding out onto the patio to join Phil.

Maria is a willow-thin South American beauty who always looks exquisite, like a model from the pages of a fashion magazine. Quietly spoken, with a huge smile framing perfect teeth, she wears long slender skirts or tailored linen slacks, with chiffon or pure cotton blouses and always a hat to cover her sleek black hair. Phil says that she has brought four large suitcases with her, and 20 wooden coat hangers.

I have never met anybody so laid back, so effortlessly elegant and so perpetually relaxed. She appears unfazed, or possibly unaware, when Phil calls her impatiently. When she eventually materialises she does so unhurriedly and with a serene smile that lights up a radius of 30 feet around her. When she cooks she does so to perfection, and serves with style meals that are nutritious, well-balanced, lovingly prepared and exquisitely presented. Every plate is a work of art. The only drawback is that it takes her so long - from when she emerges in the early afternoon until late evening to deliver the dish to the table. It can take her as long as 20 minutes to peel a single prawn, although you will never find a prawn more beautifully peeled. Where Angela can produce six perfect meals in a day, Maria is more likely to produce one perfect meal every six days. Usually Angela cooks for everybody, although Phil says he is happy feeding himself on biscuits, fruit, cups of tea and his signature dish - beans on toast. He is beginning to experiment with salads, too. Unlike George, he has little interest in food except as a source of fuel.

As different as they are from each other, both couples are ideally matched. Both the women are intelligent, gentle and easy-going, happy to sit quietly chatting and reading. The relationship between the two men is a source of constant entertainment to me. Phil's bell, which he uses to summon George, is like the one we had in Kenya when I was a child to call the house servant at meal times to clear the table. It's made of brass and shaped like a lady wearing a crinoline.

Tinkle, tinkle, is followed by heavy footsteps on the gravel, and a request to turn the pages of the newspaper, or hand him his cup of tea from the table. George, a loveable, roly-poly Buddha, is almost invariably good-humoured, although occasionally he shows small signs of rebellion.

"I've only just sat down. Why don't you leave me in peace? I've got a belly-ache."

"Self-inflicted," says Phil, unsympathetically. "The reason you have a belly-ache is because you eat too much."

"Thanks, that's made me feel better," replies George. "It's good to have friends. Angela, bring me a couple of Mars bars."

Aside from music, books and gadgets, Phil's passion is interior and garden design. He has been looking at Lavande's garden, and has a number of sketches spread out on his table.

"Er, do you mind if I make a few suggestions?" he asks. "You have some lovely plants, but they don't really stand out very well. They look a bit random, as if you haven't thought it through. If you moved them around, I think you could have a very nice garden."

I agree that not a lot of planning has gone into it. I buy things that I like and plop them wherever I can manage to gouge a hole out of the stony ground.

"For example, it would look better if those bushes were over to the side, there, so that you could see further down the garden. That corner is rather dark; if you removed those old laurels there would be far more light. Then you could put a table and chairs there to get the early morning sunshine. And those shrubs tend to block the view of the pond, and would be better on the other side. Do you see what I mean?"

What I need, I joke, is to be on one of those make-over programs.

"Hm," he murmurs, and asks whether I have a wheelbarrow, bucket, spade and fork, and tells me to leave the rest to him.

Good-natured George awoke this morning to find himself working as a jobbing gardener under Phil's direction. I hear him asking why he has to work while he's on holiday.

"Because it's good for you. You need to exercise to lose weight," Phil explains.

"Why aren't you doing some of the work?" questions George, pink with effort and heat one day. "Don't you need the exercise too?"

"I am working. It's called management. I do the thinking, and you carry it out. You are my amanuensis."

"Your what?"

"Never mind."

I am delighted at my good fortune, but mortified to know that George is working as slave labour.

"Don't you worry, doll," he says, "I'm happy doin' it for you." He chuckles.

"Ask him to tell you," says Phil one day, as we stand watching George barrowing sacks of bark down to the new ornamental flowerbed Phil has designed, "what happened to the greenhouse."

George throws his fork onto the ground, and sighs. "Why do you always want to drag up that story, Phil?" he asks.

"Because it's a good one, and it illustrates why you deserve the title of Captain Calamity."

George sighs, smiles, opens a packet of chocolate biscuits, and calls for Angela to pour him a cup of tea. As he sips and munches, he tells his story.

"Well, there's this old bird - wealthy, she is - who lived next door to us. She had this damn great garden – fu**ing, sorry, I mean bloody enormous, but the whole patch had gone to weeds and she couldn't get to her greenhouse any more. It was a big one – one of those wooden framed jobs, about 15ft. long. She asked me to clear the place up for her. So I went down with the strimmer, but it was all nettles and brambles. I spent all morning and I wasn't making much impression, so I had a good idea. I tipped petrol all over the weeds, stood back and threw a lighted paper. And whoosh! There was no more weeds."

Both men roar with laughter.

"Or greenhouse," Phil reminds him.

"Er, yes, now you come to mention it." George munches a fistful of biscuits. "First of all, the explosion blew out every pane of glass. That was bad enough. And then there was this crackly noise. The frame caught fire and went up, or should I say down, in less than five minutes. So the old lady's lovely greenhouse was no more. Instead she had a great big black space and a garden full of shattered glass. She never asked me to do anything for her again."

"That's why you need me to direct you," Phil reminds him.

"Yeah. You just sit there and watch, sunshine. Why don't we talk about when you was in banking?" He calls out to Angela to ask her to make a couple of bacon sarnies. My ears prick up. Phil doesn't look like any banker I've ever seen, and I sense there could be a good story here. I look questioningly at Phil, but he just points to the newly-made flowerbed and says, "Look, you've left a stone unturned there."

In just four days Phil's design and George's hard work have transformed the garden, and now all it needs is copious watering, because this is the worst possible time of year to be uprooting and transplanting trees and shrubs. We find a perforated hosepipe and snake it around and leave the tap running slowly all night. After their initial bewilderment, the plants slowly perk up and are definitely more suited to their new situations.

Phil is merciless in his teasing of George. Now the gardening project is finished, he suggests they should go running together each morning.

"Are you joking? Can you really imagine me being able to run ten miles? I'd be dead after fifty feet. And haven't you done enough to me already? This was meant to be a holiday, and all I've done is work."

"And eat," Phil reminds him. "Anyway, it's good for you. You need to do something to burn off all that fat."

George grins and tells him to bugger off.

So this morning I am very surprised to see him walking in the direction of the village, which is over a mile away. Angela says that he has decided to take a "daily constitutional" to the bakery to collect their lunchtime baguettes. She's delighted to see him getting some exercise, but it's strange, she says, because he would normally drive a hundred feet rather than walk. Maybe it's something in the lovely country air. Two hours later he ambles in with a baguette under each arm, saying he feels fitter already and has thoroughly enjoyed himself strolling along and enjoying the scenery.

He's going to do it every day while they're here. Even Phil is impressed, and says he'll go with George, who resists firmly and slightly irritably.

"No, I want to get away from you. Allow me a little peace once in a while, will you?"

"I bet you don't do it," says Phil.

But he does, setting off determinedly every morning at 10.00am, fuelled by a hearty breakfast. "It's so good for George," Angela says. "I worry about his weight. I really hope he'll keep up walking when we're back home."

On their final morning here Angela and Phil are hard at work cleaning their cottages. George has taken one last stroll to the bakery, and Maria is OMMMMMing from the bedroom. Their car is loaded, the engine running, and Phil is drumming his fingers on the door. Maria appears in a slinky multi-coloured wrap-around skirt and a tiny black sun top. She smells delicious and looks radiant.

"Did you clean the bathroom?" Phil asks.

She smiles in a puzzled way. "What?"

Phil sighs softly and vanishes into Lavande. Ten minutes later he reappears with an armful of wet towels harvested from the bathroom, and the twenty wooden coat hangers Maria has forgotten in the wardrobe.

They drive away leaving two spotless cottages, a newly-landscaped garden, and a very large space in my life. I miss Elvis, Roy, Ricky, Buddy and Neil; I miss Angela's sweet nature and Maria's glamour and serenity; I miss the sound of Phil's newspaper pages rustling and his banter with George; I miss the laughter and the meals we have shared. And I miss the sound of that small tinkling bell.

A couple of weeks later I meet Katherine, the village baker's wife, and she mentions George.

"Charmant! Très amusant! Et quelle voix!"

"He sang for you?"

"Mais oui! It was wonderful! He was very good for our business - people came every day to listen to him. And how he loved our cakes!"

"Cakes?"

"Yes, every day he bought two baguettes, three éclairs and three chaussons aux pommes."

I am laughing as I drive home, thinking of George busily eating all those cakes as he took his daily slimming exercise.

Chapter Thirty
Year Four – Worrying Unnecessarily

MY long-stay American guests are due today. It had been a bit of a preoccupation working out how to explain to Ivy that they will not be needing her services, and I'd been rehearsing ways of breaking the news. With her personality ranging from murderous to suicidal, I couldn't imagine what a horrible scene she was going to create. So I could not have been more astonished, or delighted, when she phoned me three weeks ago to say that she needed an urgent meeting with me as she had some bad news and some good news. I hoped that she wasn't going to batter me with more tales of tragic and miserable events that had overtaken people she knows.

She arrived dressed in a Garboesque outfit of black pencil skirt, white blouse tied at the neck in a large floppy bow and a wide-brimmed black felt hat. A grey wool stole dangled around her neck and a pair of enormous sunglasses perched on her nose. Her thick blonde hair fell over her collar.

She was radiant and effusive.

"Sit down, darling," she gushed, pointing me to one of my own armchairs.

"Good or bad first?" she asked.

"Let's get the worst over, shall we?"

"Yes, let's. The thing is, darling, I feel frightful about it, but I'm going to have to let you down." I mentally compute the significance of this. Will I be worse, or better off? I raise my eyebrows and look curious.

"I should really have warned you sooner, I know, but I dared not say anything until I knew – never tempt the Fates. You see – and this is the good news! – I auditioned for the lead in a theatrical production a few weeks ago – against fierce competition, I might add - and yesterday I learned that I have been chosen for the part. Can you imagine? I've been waiting most of my life to be a star, and finally my moment has arrived. I know that you'll understand that I must grasp this opportunity greedily, selfishly, because who knows where it could lead? We all know that opportunity knocks but once. Talent scouts are everywhere, incognito, just like the Michelin restaurant inspectors. It's a huge chance for me." She clasps her hands to her chest.

I tried to look simultaneously pleased for her and disappointed that she wouldn't be around here for a while.

"How long will the play run for?"

She opened a handbag and produced a long cigarette holder and a pack of Sobranie Black Russian cigarettes. She stuck one into the holder, then held it elegantly in her hand without lighting it.

"Initially we're giving two performances at the beginning of September. Then there is every chance that we will go on tour. My producer will be making all those arrangements in due course. So you'll realise that with rehearsals my time is going to be totally taken up."

She stood up and tossed her head back, throwing out one arm theatrically, as if addressing an unseen audience.

She was sacrificing two months of work for two nights of glory, but that would work so well for me that I wanted to scramble onto the rooftop and scream 'Hallelujah!' at the top of my voice.

Instead I said, "Well, all I can do is congratulate you! Of course, I'll miss you." That was true, although probably not in the way she imagined.

"I'm sure you'll manage perfectly well without me," she said, putting the cigarette and its holder back into her bag. Slinging the stole around her shoulders, she stalked to the door.

"I'll do my best," I promised.

Over the last year Annie, the Americans' spokeswoman and organiser and I have been writing back and forth debating how to find room for all of them. What we've agreed is that they will take over the house and both cottages, and I'll go and live in a tent at the local campsite, taking one of our dogs with me. He's sick, and I couldn't leave him with anybody. I want him with me all the time. They will look after the house, the garden and the animals, and I'll be "on holiday." However, Cindy, our old Welsh cob is now chronically lame, so I'll be coming back every day to administer Bute and aspirin in toasted jam sandwiches, which is how she likes it.

Annie has two concerns: one is finding the right blend of coffee for her father, Sam, and the second is ensuring medical care for her mother Jessie, who has been having treatment for two years for diverticulitis. I reassure her they can confidently rely on our local doctor, who speaks fluent English, and French medical care is right up there at the top of the league. But when it comes to the coffee question, I am at a bit of a loss, not being much of a connoisseur myself. A spoonful of instant powder in a mug is just as good as anything else for me. However I have been to the local supermarkets and counted over 40 different labels so I'm confident we'll be able to find one that will suit Sam. Another consideration, says Annie, is that her two teenage daughters like to change their clothes several times a day. Do we have an electric dryer? In my mind I see the electricity meter spinning dizzily 24 hours a day, leading to bankruptcy and ruin, because energy costs in the United States bear no comparison to those in Europe. Happily, our dryer had long since rusted away in the outhouse where we had put it after using it for a few weeks and receiving the electricity bill, so I can reply truthfully that we don't own one, but dry our laundry in the sunshine.

I admit I've been feeling apprehensive about the teenagers after Ticia and Lesley. My impression of American teenagers up to now has only been through the small or large screen, where they seem to be loud, demanding, gum-chewing and sex-crazed, so I have awaited Diana and Allie with some trepidation. In fact I'm very nervous about the whole project. While both cottages are comfortable and modern, our own house is still quite primitive. For instance, my kitchen is a collection of rickety old units balanced on breeze-blocks. The shower cubicle in the bathroom is tiny and the sliding door keeps falling off. There's no staircase leading up to the loft where I've managed to get two beds and a rickety table set up. You have to climb up a woodwormy ladder, of which one rung is dangerously thin, and there's no ceiling – just the rafters and undersides of the tiles. And LOTS of spiders. The floorboards are rough and wobbly. Cables snake all over the place to supply electricity to various machines and lighting. I'm getting more and more worried. About the electricity in the house. About the safety of the water. About the height of the beams in

Pissenlit. About the comfort of the beds. About insects. About everything. I'm a nervous wreck, lying awake for long nights worrying about what to worry about next. How are my new American friends going to cope? Will they take one look and run screaming back to Oklahoma? Waiting for their arrival I feel sick, but as soon as they step out of their hired car there's a huge whoosh of relief. They are the happiest, most easy-going and enthusiastic people you could wish to meet. And the two girls are a true delight. Polite, confident, helpful and instantly at home.

Annie is a teacher, Jim a geologist. As the vanguard they are going to arrange everything for the rest of the group who will be arriving over the next few days. When I tell Annie that I'm a little concerned her parents will find life in rural France rather primitive, she tells me they are intrepid senior citizens who have hiked in the Himalayas, ridden elephants through the Indian jungle, toured the Arctic circle on a whale-watching boat, and ridden camels round the Pyramids. They are bringing friends with them – an architect and his interior designer wife, plus Annie's sister and an aunt, bringing their party up to ten.

The two girls select, for their accommodation, the spider-ridden loft, and set about organising it with much laughter, picking bunches of herbs, wild flowers and grasses and sticking them into jam jars and bottles which they dot around the house. Annie has brought with her a whole suitcase full of books, which Jim drags out of the car and up the stairs to my room, where they are going to stay. I introduce them to the animals – they're fine with all of them except the cats, which I notice they shoo away gently but firmly. Oh dear, I hope the cats won't take umbrage. At least it's very hot and there are plenty of places for them to sleep, but they've always slept on our bed and sat on our laps, so they're in for a bit of a shock.

Late afternoon Annie asks if I can show her where to shop, so we drive to one of the supermarkets where she stocks up her trolley. When we arrive at the coffee section, she asks which brand I recommend for her father. Well, I say, I really can't give any advice, I usually buy the instant coffee with added dried milk. She takes a tin to try, although I can't imagine that a real coffee drinker is going to be too impressed.

We eat together, early, then, leaving them with a small booklet on how things work, where to find things and how to deal with the various idiosyncrasies of our animals and electricity, I take my dog and my leave. As our guests will be using my car, a friend has kindly lent me an old banger so that I can get back and forth. The campsite is two miles away. It's a small site beside a winding river, with about half a dozen other campers scattered around. With a pile of books, a small stove, a cool box and my dog for company, I settle down for the night.

Next morning, when I go back Annie and Jim are enjoying breakfast in the sun, and the girls are sweeping out the barn. They're so perfectly relaxed and at home that I know I can stop worrying. Despite my initial misgivings Allie and Diana are enraptured with their bedroom and not all fazed by the spiders. Allie, I discover, is a great organiser. She's written out charts showing what times the animals are fed, what they are given, and where it's kept. All the gardening tools that I tend to leave wherever I last used them are now arranged in an orderly row in one of the barns. Now she's writing out a shopping list.

Annie claps her hands. "Grecian urns," she calls.

Facing each other, the two girls hook their right arms together, raise their left arms languidly, and lean back gracefully, then nearly fall over backwards, giggling.

"They were in a school play," explains their mother. "Cast as Grecian urns." Forever after, that is how I shall remember the girls.

Satisfied that they have settled in comfortably, I say I'll see them again in a few days to check that all is well. In case of emergency, they know where to find me at the campsite. I can get to our field to doctor Cindy without going near the house. Most of the time I sit reading, my dog lying at my feet. I'm waiting for biopsy results for him, and in my heart and stomach I know it's going to be very bad news. These will be our last days together, and I want them to be as special as possible for him. He's enjoying having all my attention, and at night he stretches out beside my sleeping back, his spine pressed against mine, his head beside my pillow.

The other six visitors arrive at the end of the week. Annie's parents, Allie senior and Douglas are a lively couple in their early seventies. Douglas is a retired political journalist from Arkansas, slim, tall and stooped, with an unruly head of silver hair; Allie senior is a well-built, no-nonsense lady. With their close friends, handsome Dieter and elegant, blonde Laura, they move into Lavande, while Douglas's sister Nan, and Annie's sister Meg share Pissenlit.

Often, at their invitation I spend a few hours with them all, and am slowly adapting to their strange cuisine. Marshmallows and brownie, chocolate broken into pieces sits on the table next to cheese, chicken salad, or burgers. And Douglas has found the coffee that suits him perfectly – the instant stuff with dried milk powder that I drink!

Dieter and Douglas have begun to mend the archaic fencing that is falling down. I can hear them laughing as they collect fallen branches and lengths of baling twine that they weave together ingeniously to form barricades to keep the dogs in the garden and the horses out of it. The girls get a huge kick from drying their laundry by hanging it on a line in the sun. They love the clean fresh smell. Allie senior says that as a young woman she had always dried her washing like that, Annie and the girls have only ever used an electric dryer.

Apart from a single tornado, the weather is hot and sunny all day every day, and the grass is high and dry. The mower can't cope with it, so at their request I buy a scythe. The teenagers take turns slashing the grass down into hay and feeding it to the horses. All the guests are enjoying a glimpse into a world that is so different from their lives in busy American cities.

Going back to the tornado for just a moment: I'm lying on the grass outside my tent, reading. It is a warm day with a slight breeze. Abruptly the sky darkens and the air becomes still. I put my book down and stand up, and in the time it takes to do so the sky turns completely black, as black as night. There is a whistling noise, and the trees begin to sway. I put the dog in the car, and drive to the house. As we arrive torrential rain starts falling. Thunder and lightning crash and flash all around. The ground is several inches deep in water and rain is pouring into the dining room through the roof. There's nobody here; the guests have all gone out for lunch. Within a few minutes the storm has passed and the sun returns. I mop up the water from the floor and drive back to the campsite.

Beside the river there had been a copse of poplar trees. They have all been snapped in half and lie in tangled heaps on the ground. My tent has collapsed, two carbon fibre poles are broken. All around tents are lying in puddles and campers are sploshing around draping their belongings over hedges and fences. Miraculously the inside of my tent is dry and I manage to re-erect it, somewhat lopsidedly. In a couple of hours everything is dry and back to normal. Later that evening I go home to give Cindy her medication, and ask the guests whether they had been caught in the storm – they had only gone to the town six miles away for lunch. What storm, they ask. They hadn't even seen a cloud.

Allie senior went to town today on her own for what she describes as a small adventure – a shopping trip to a supermarket. She speaks almost no French, apart from the numbers 1-10, but she has promised to cook her famous meatloaf and has made up her mind to find the ingredients herself. When she returns a couple of hours later, she is shaking with laughter and heaving two heavy carrier bags.

"I pointed to the ground beef," she laughs, "and the man asked did I want one kilo. Well, I didn't know how much a kilo was - I guessed about 4 ounces - so I shook my head and told him four kilos. I just couldn't believe it when he started shovelling all this beef into bags." One kilo equals two-and-a-quarter pounds.

She's baked multiple batches of meatloaf and frozen them. "We aren't ever going to be able use all this," she says. But she's wrong.

Chapter Thirty-One
Year Four – The Nudity Clinic

WHEN my mobile phone rings at 8.00am, and I see that it's Douglas calling, I know there's a crisis.

He is the most gentle, courteous man, and apologises for calling so early, but Allie is in trouble. She's in terrible pain, and needs to see the doctor.

Allie senior has been up all night. The medication she has been prescribed in the States has done nothing to help, and she is bent double with pain. She's a tough, stoic lady, but her face is drawn and grey. I take her straight to our doctor, who has more charm than any one man deserves and speaks flawless English. Allie comes out from his office shaking her head. "He says I don't have diverticulitis. That's real strange. I have to go this afternoon to have an X-ray." She has a prescription for a pain killer, which works quickly, and I drive her to the clinic after lunch. When she emerges she's looking stunned.

"I can't believe what happened," she says.

"They sent me into a small cubicle, and I had to undress and put on a white gown. Then I walked out of another door in the cubicle into a room where the X-ray machine is. There were two doctors there, and they asked me to remove the gown. I was standing there naked in a room with two men! In the States that would never happen – we'd sue!"

"Well," I tell her. "I know what you mean. In England, there would normally be a female nurse present, but here in France they do things a little differently."

"They sure do," she laughs.

We return to the doctor straight away with the X-rays. He reads the report, looks at the plates, and picks up the phone.

"Go back to the clinic tomorrow. I've made an appointment for you for an ultra-sound scan at 10.45. Don't worry, you are going to be OK."

All the friends and family are anxious, but Allie insists that they enjoy their holiday and don't worry about her.

So next morning we return to what Allie has christened the Nudity Clinic, and she does her stripping act again, and back we go to the doctor once more with the scans.

"Madame," he says, "as I told you, you certainly do not have diverculitis. But you do have a kidney stone, and you need to have it removed. Very quickly." He picks up his phone and calls the hospital in Poitiers. "They will expect you at 2.00." It is 12.45.

We rush home, collect Douglas and some toiletries and a nightie, and drive to Poitiers, where Allie is welcomed into the clinic. I am so impressed by her calm acceptance of what is happening to her, in a foreign country. She is interested in everything around her, and not apparently in any way alarmed.

Once she's settled in her room, the anaesthetist comes to see her. He wants to know her medical history, any medication she takes, her age, height and weight. Allie tells me how many pounds she weighs. There is a slight panic as I try to remember how to convert pounds into kilograms. The anaesthetist gives her hand a squeeze, tells her to enjoy her stay, and says he looks forward to seeing her early next morning. When he has left the room, Allie sends Douglas to find some coffee, and the moment he has left the room she says urgently: "Listen, I've done something really bad! I've lied about my weight. I don't want Douglas to know how much I really weigh, so I've taken off a couple of stone. But now I'm scared - because they may not give me enough stuff to knock me out. Can you speak to the anaesthetist for me?"

I find a nurse, who takes me to the anaesthetist, and I explain about Allie's predicament. He smiles gently, and tells me: "Madame - tell her not to worry. It is normal. Ladies very often underestimate their weight, but we have a very good idea of how much they actually weigh." There is a twinkle in his eye.

By the time I get back to Allie's room Douglas has returned from his errand. I nod to Allie and give her a thumbs up behind his back. We stay with her for a couple of hours, chatting until her evening meal arrives, then I drive Douglas home and stay for a meal.

I phone the clinic next morning, and they report that Allie is conscious and recovering from her operation. We drive up to see her, and she's cheerful, pain-free and relieved. The surgeon told her that in another 24 hours she would most likely have lost her kidney. She's impressed with the French medical system, even if their etiquette is a little lax.

"I was lying on the table in a small room, after the operation, with just a short gown which only reached my hips. The door opened and a young man put his head round and asked if I was feeling OK. Then the anaesthetist came to ask if I was OK. And there I was naked from the waist down!"

After Douglas and I collect her from the hospital next day, I take my beautiful dog for his appointment at the vet. It is the news I was expecting and my heart breaks as I bring him home to bury him. All our pets are special, but sometimes one is a little more special than the others, and he was. I don't want to spoil our guests' day, so I manage to put on a calm face and even stay to eat with them. They had come to love him too, and we all sit in a circle in the garden and they say a few words for him. Unlike me, they are devout Christians, but they keep their religion to themselves, and just send blessings to my lovely boy.

That night I lie in my tent weeping and weeping, until my body feels as if there's not a single tear left in it.

Chapter Thirty-Two
Year Four – The Great Meatloaf Deterrent

DIETER, Laura, Nan and Meg left a few days ago. They are travelling to various other parts of Europe to visit friends, and today Annie, Jim and the girls are leaving. Jim has to go back to work, and Annie must prepare for the forthcoming term. I'm going to miss them, because I've become very fond of them all, especially the girls. They're travelling to Paris by train from Poitiers, and almost miss the train because Annie has misread the ticket. Suddenly we've lost a whole hour, and there is a massive scramble from the breakfast table, to get their things into the car and get them to the station on time. With frantic hugs and kisses they say their farewells to Douglas and Allie senior, who are staying on for another couple of weeks. We cram into my car and rush to the station. Little Allie is sobbing, because she had planned their departure meticulously and now it's all gone wrong and it's a muddle. We arrive at the station with less than five minutes to catch the train, but Annie's suitcase of books is so heavy, there's no lift, and it takes all of us two journeys to manhandle all the luggage out of the car and into the station. Little Allie can barely breathe for crying, and we're six minutes late by the time we haul the last suitcase onto the platform. The station loudspeaker goes "boing" (it's a kind of melodious noise that precedes announcements,) and regrets that the train from Bordeaux to Paris has been unavoidably delayed by 25 minutes. Time for us all to catch our breath, and for Little Allie to regain her composure before I wave them away and return home to live back in my house.

Now that there are just the two of them, Allie and Douglas are keen to do some sight-seeing. Our country roads are terrifyingly narrow until you've driven on them for a few months, and Allie is a nervous passenger when Douglas is driving. "Douglas, there's a bicycle ahead," she warns. "Honey, be careful, there's a car coming towards us." "Mind the bend, Douglas."

Douglas, who is the most tolerant and gentle gentleman obligingly brings the car to a halt at every warning, and never goes faster than 25 mph, nor does he get above second gear. Every journey with him at the wheel is a tense ordeal for them both, but Allie seems to have confidence in me and likes me to drive them, so they invite me to be their chauffeur and we spend many enjoyable days exploring the region's attractions. We visit many of the Loire châteaux, explore Poitiers, have a heavenly day at Villandry, and go out most days for lunch. Douglas is adventurous in his tastes, and ready to eat anything, but Allie is far more cautious and nearly fell off her chair when she saw brains on the menu. Generally she ends up with a steak and fries, while Douglas seeks out the most "French foreign" dish on the menu. When he wants to order tongue, Allie puts her foot down with a firm hand. "Douglas – you're not eating that." So he has stuffed heart instead.

One day when I'm committed elsewhere they go out to lunch at a local hotel, and Allie wants to know what she should order that will be "safe." I suggest the mushroom omelette - omelette aux cêpes. When I see them that evening, I ask how they enjoyed their meal. Much to Allie's disgust, Douglas had eaten lamb, but she had taken my advice and had the omelette. It was nice enough, she said, except that there were small pieces of something brown and rubbery in it, which she thought might be pieces of liver, so she had carefully cut them all out. They were the mushrooms, I explained. "Well, they didn't look like the kind of mushrooms we have," she replied.

All that meat loaf is just about to come in handy. There is an Englishman living in the village who keeps calling around to see Douglas and Allie every night

"He's a real interesting guy," says Douglas, "but how do you let him know when it's time for him to go home?"

"How do you mean?" I ask.

"Well, he comes over every evening about 8.30pm. That was OK just once, but we like to go to bed by 9.00pm." Douglas and Allie are early risers - they like to watch the sun come up each day.

"The first night he came I gave him a whisky, and we chewed the cud for a couple of hours. Allie went up to bed, but I sat there with him until near midnight. I had to ask him to excuse me."

"Then he came back the next evening at the same time, and he just talked and talked, and smoked his pipe. Allie went up to bed at 9.00pm, and I stood up, but he just sat there and poured another drink. It's kind of hard to get away from him."

When I see the neighbour next day, he says he's very sorry for Douglas, whose wife is such a bore and goes to bed at 9.00pm, so he's taken to spending the evenings with him to keep him entertained. I tell him that they both go to bed early because they get up at 5.30am, but he just grunts and shuffles back to his house.

The next night Douglas tries different tactics to dislodge the neighbour. When darkness falls, he does not switch on the lights, and the two of them sit talking in the pitch dark as if it was a perfectly natural thing to do. The following night Douglas asks him what he'd like to drink, and he replies he'll have the same as Douglas.

"I'm having water," Douglas says, and solemnly puts a bottle of water and two glasses on the table. Allie has gone to bed early to avoid the visitor for whom she is beginning to develop a rare dislike. The two men sit in the dark, drinking water.

Still he comes back the following night, but Allie has prepared a surprise for him.

"You must have some of our meatloaf," she says, handing him a huge slice on a plate. And when his plate is empty, she slaps another lump on. The chewing keeps him quiet, and when Allie clears away the plates Douglas stands up to help her, and between them they spend quite a long time in the kitchen washing up, leaving the visitor sitting alone, with nothing to drink and nobody to talk to.

When he returns the next evening, Allie has set a place for him at the table. "We eat at 6.00pm, because we like to go to bed by 8.30pm, but I know you enjoyed my meatloaf, so here's some more for you." He munches his way through it, washing it down with water.

The next evening he is back again. Allie is already in bed, and Douglas is in his pyjamas, but there's a fresh plate of meatloaf for the visitor who is plainly deaf and blind to all the heavy hints being hurled at him. He protests that he doesn't want to disturb them, but Douglas is quietly insistent, so another lump of meatloaf is chewed, swallowed, washed down with water as Douglas

242

sits politely, benignly watching the meatloaf disappear. When he stands up to leave, Douglas invites him back the next day, because there is still plenty of meatloaf in the freezer.

But the following evening there is no sign of him. "My meatloaf mountain deterrent certainly came in very handy," laughs Allie. "It finally got rid of that unwanted guest!"

Douglas and Allie's visit comes to an end and I drive them to the station to catch their train back to Paris before they fly home. These happy, kind people have become like family to me, and leave a large space behind them. And a couple of meatloaves in the freezer.

The next time I see the neighbour he mentions that my guests are very odd people.

"All they seem to do is eat meatloaf, and sleep," he mutters. "Still - Americans. What can you expect?"

Chapter Thirty-Three

Year Four – The Beginning Of The End

WALKING the dogs, I have been having several long thinks. The last four years have been an interesting experience, and I've met some wonderful people, learned a great deal about human nature, and made some lifelong friends. I've had many laughs and some moments of despair. But as so many others were finding last year, times are changing. The Pound has weakened further against the Euro, and France is no longer a country where you can eat out cheaply. Fuel prices have shot up. Holidaymakers are choosing cheaper destinations in Eastern Europe and North Africa where they are guaranteed sunshine. Our area is now flooded with holiday cottages as buyers have snapped up and developed properties into rental accommodation. Weather-wise last year was a disastrous summer. The holiday season is brief, from mid-June to the end of August. Without Brad's friends booking eight weeks, this would have been a very poor year. Competition for guests is fierce, and the new properties have heated swimming pools and jacuzzis and a higher standard of facilities than we can offer.

After two calamitous winter bookings in Pissenlit, I've decided not to take any more, and – taking into account the income against the outgoings – advertising, insurance, maintenance, taxes, Ivy's wages, it hardly justifies keeping going. I'm getting physically tired, too. My energy level is low. I'm struggling to look after all the animals, a large house and garden as well as the cottages on my own, whilst my husband works in England.

I've taken down the website and cancelled our advertising for next year.

Ivy comes round, dressed as a gendarme, selling tickets to the amateur dramatic production in which she has the starring role. She's in a rush because there's a huge demand and she's not even certain if there will be enough tickets to go round. They might have to put on an extra night. I buy two tickets and invite Fliss to join me for the event in a fortnight's time. I should let Ivy know that there won't be any work for her here next year, but it would be a shame to rain on her parade, so I'll wait until after the play.

I haven't heard from Tristram for a couple of months, and although I've rung him several times his phone is never answered. I start to worry, and drive over, through the forest that now seems sinister. The children greet me with their normal enthusiasm, but Tristram looks dreadful and they cluster around his legs anxiously. There are boxes and piles of kitchen equipment, books, clothes all over the living room, pictures stacked up against the walls.

"What's happening?" I ask.

"I'm moving out."

"Where?"

"I've rented a place in Brittany. I can't stay here. I hate this bloody house." His face is twisted with anger and misery. "And I can't sell it unless I can find Beverly. It's in joint names."

Beverly's garden is a tangle of weeds and withered flowers.

"Any chance of a mint tea?" I ask.

He smiles bitterly. "Help yourself."

I can't find the kettle, but there's an open bottle of Pouilly-Fuissé, and I pour a couple of glasses.

"Can I help?" I ask, as he shoves piles of books into boxes.

He shakes his head. "Nobody can help. Nobody can help. I'd really prefer to be alone, if you don't mind." What can I say? I stroke Pumpkin's silky head and walk out of the house. Driving away I glance in the rear-view mirror, remembering my first visit, when Tristram and Beverly stood in the doorway waving me away. Now the doorway is empty, the house looks shabby and has lost its glow.

A near-disaster in Pissenlit. A couple of young men are staying there, and have complained of being cold. It's the beginning of September, and still very mild. But for people used to living in a centrally-heated environment I realise that our idea of cold and theirs are not the same. Because they are very pleasant, and I want them to be happy, I've given them a supply of logs, kindling and some firelighters.

It's around midnight and I'm asleep when there's a loud banging on the door and a lot of shouting.

"Quick! We're on fire!"

Pissenlit is tropical. It's like a sauna. There is putrid smoke everywhere and the floor is soaking.

They have stoked the woodburner up to such a temperature that it has set fire to the ceiling, which looks pretty with little clusters of red embers sparkling and glowing over it. The cast iron of the fire is glowing red, and they've tried to kill the flames by throwing water all over it, which has merely created steam and smoke.

We open all the windows, bang the ceiling with wet towels and tip sand over the wood until the fire goes out. The ceiling is charred and the walls are blackened.

They apologise profusely. "We wanted to see how hot it could get," explained one of them. "Of course, we'll pay for the damage."

Which they do, but they have to leave the next day because the place reeks of smoke, everywhere is covered in soot, and Lavande is occupied. Grrr. Later I will find that the cold water they threw on the wood burner had cracked it. Just as well we won't be needing it next year.

Fliss, who has reverted to the woolly tights, boots and mini skirt, and I go to watch Ivy on the opening night of her play. It isn't quite what we'd been expecting, taking place in a chilly village hall where we sit on low little chairs borrowed from the primary school. As the hall fills with both English and French, sipping red wine from plastic cups, the crowd of bodies heats up the room. There is an air of merriment and anticipation. Every so often a face peers through a crack in the curtain, as some member of the cast looks out. A French comedian comes on and tells some jokes. My French is not good enough to catch the finer points, but from the rapturous reception given to him by the French part of the audience, and the roars of laughter, it seems as if he is a great success. A group of little people come and recite rhymes. They are earnest and confident, and absolutely endearing. Some older children give a demonstration of line-dancing with great gusto and yeehaws. During the interval there is much supping of red wine and munching of peanuts before we take our little low seats. An expectant hush falls. We hear some frantic whispering, a familiar voice screeching, and then the curtain opens.

It's a typical French farce, and very funny. Husbands and lovers hiding in cupboards, gasps, rolling eyes, slamming doors. And then Ivy steps onto the stage. To our surprise she does not have a leading role, but is playing a waitress, clearing away and mopping tables. The lighting and her costume cruelly show every sag and wrinkle. A very short tight skirt and very high heels exaggerate her short, stocky legs. "Oh dear!" says Fliss with a wry smile. Still, Ivy throws herself into her part with the confidence of Maggie Smith. She hums loudly and keeps smiling at the audience, raising a coy eyebrow and positioning herself in front of the couple sitting at the table, the leading players in the production, who look startled and raise their voices to be heard over her humming. The audience roar with uncertain laughter. Is this part of the play, or is Ivy trying to upstage the others?

When the curtain comes down on the scene, angry voices can be heard backstage, and it sounds as if something heavy like a ladder has fallen down. There's a long wait before the curtain comes up on the next scene, in which a different person is playing the part of the waitress. After the cast have taken a final bow, they join the audience in the bar. There is a distinct chill between Ivy, the producer and the rest of the cast, but she is still oozing confidence and offering her autograph to anybody who looks at her. She orders Fliss and I to keep our eyes open in the newspapers for reviews over the coming week.

Chapter Thirty-Four
Year Four – The Final Curtain

THE holiday season is almost over, with just a handful of bookings left. Pissenlit is out of action due to the smoke damage, but luckily there are vacancies in Lavande so I can fit everybody in.

Ivy has been subdued since the night of the play, and I can't help feeling for her. She had built her hopes up so high. I think she really had believed that her part in a tiny rural village production might lead to greater things. And I still haven't told her that her job is coming to an end. When she's finished for today I'll open a bottle of wine and break the news as gently as I can. I've collected a pile of clothes and odds and ends to give her to cheer her up.

Today she's wearing disappointingly conventional clothes, a brown skirt and baggy jumper; her eyes are puffy, and her mouth is pinched angrily.

"Is everything OK?" I ask.

"Nothing is fucking OK. The oil warning light on my car is on permanently, and the neighbours are throwing stones at my windows."

The man who lives next door to us is a motor mechanic, and I ask him if he'll have a look at the oil gauge. He drives the car for five minutes and reports that there's nothing wrong. There is no red light.

"Look!" yells Ivy. "Look – there – can't you see it, you fool!?" She jabs her finger at the dashboard.

"That's not a light. It's the warning area. It's just red paint."

"Well it's never been there before," snaps Ivy.

"I'm sorry, but it has. It's only paint. There's nothing wrong with your car, really."

But he can't convince her, and shaking his head he leaves her pulling faces behind his back.

"Idiot," she says loudly.

As she's clearly in a very bad mood, I leave her to tidy up in Lavande while I go out into the garden to pull up the weeds. I'm psyching myself up to tell her there's no more work for her after the end of this month.

I hear a loud clatter followed by a shriek.

"Fucking filthy bastard swine," she roars.

She appears in the doorway, scarlet with rage, the wattles on her neck a violent shade of purple. "That's it! You can keep your fucking money. I wasn't born to be a skivvy. And I'm not paid to deal with turds!"

Taking a deep breath, I tentatively squeeze past her into the cottage. Water is trickling down the stairs from the overturned bucket at the top. Loo cleaner, bathroom spray, sponges and part-used loo rolls are scattered all over the floor.

"What exactly has happened?" I ask.

"What do you think, you ignorant cow!? One of your filthy guests in your shabby building has left a huge turd in the lavatory! Absolutely disgusting."

"Oh dear. Nasty. But can't you just flush it away?"

She jumps up and down in a little Indian war dance.

All trace of the cultivated accent has vanished, and she's spouting obscenities. "Flush it yourself! Do your own dirty work, you snooty cow. Think yourself too grand to clean your own mess. Well you can just go and fuck yourself."

She spins around angrily, snatching up her handbag and heading towards the door, but somehow getting her legs crossed and ending up in an angry heap on the floor. I stoop to help her up, a spitting, cursing heap of fury. Angrily she punches at my knees and heaves herself upright. Her hair is skewed sideways, and I stare in astonishment as the glossy golden waves slither onto her right shoulder. "AAAAAAAArrrrrrrrghhhhh!" She grabs the blonde wig and jams it back over the sparse grey spikes sprouting from her head, kicking out furiously at a chair and grabbing her handbag.

Running to her car she leaves a vapour trail of rage and gin. Before I can stop her she has reversed into a wooden post, denting her rear bumper, ground into gear and taken off in a shower of flying gravel and squealing tyres.

I'm shaking, sick, horrified, overwhelmed with pity and also flooded with relief. Ivy's terminated her employment, saving me the trauma, and this time it's final. I try not to listen to the voice in my head that is chanting: "Every cloud has a silver lining." As I begin clearing up the mess, I wonder what had happened to make her become the person she is. In her own bizarre way, she's trying to make the best of a life that plainly hasn't been easy.

I find a greeting card showing a pair of mournful angels and put a cheque in with a note wishing her good luck. Funnily enough, I'm going to miss her madness.

My last guest is Sarah, an ambitious single mother who has built up her own business. Now a major British company wants to buy it and she's trying to decide whether to accept the offer. It would, she says, make her very wealthy, but on the other hand it's something she has created herself and she's reluctant to let it go. Her pretty 10-year-old daughter Frances has a mind like a sponge and an unquenchable thirst for knowledge. She's a bright little girl and loves coming with me to walk the dogs and feed the chickens. She's a pleasure to have around, and leaves behind several portraits of the animals, and one of me. It has one arm considerably longer than the other and very close-together eyes, but is easily recognisable because it has my name written on it.

Before they leave I invite Sarah to share a bottle of champagne as our final guest. It's a strange moment. I'm both relieved, and a little sad. So many interesting people have stayed with us, and I'll miss the frisson of excitement that each arrival brought, the many laughs and the occasional dramas. Between them they have left me a heart full of memories, a drawer full of mementoes, a fridge full of jars of jam and enough black pepper to fill the hold of a ship.

While Pissenlit is attached to our main house and is too tiny to serve as a permanent residence, Lavande is a good size, with its own garden, and will make a comfortable holiday home for somebody. The market is buoyant and I don't think we'll have much difficulty in finding a buyer. Still, the prospect of having neighbours is something we need to think about carefully and we are going to be very selective whom we sell to.

I go through the guest books and dig out the contact details for selected guests, and send them an email saying that Lavande will be coming up for sale soon, so if by chance they know anybody who might be interested, please point them our way.

24 hours later, we've found a buyer.

They've been thinking about buying a holiday home for several years – in fact during their last stay with us they'd viewed several properties. They are looking for somewhere that is private but not isolated, and Lavande would suit them perfectly.

Within a month, they've signed the compromis, and eight weeks later the deal is done. Lavande's new owners will use the cottage two or three times a year for their holidays.

As soon as the paperwork is signed they move in. The chickens are at their door straight away. It's too cold for gin and tonics, so there are no lemon slices, but they're thrilled with the bacon rinds. Despite the chilly December weather, our new neighbours are still happily gardening in the buff. Personally if I was dealing with the spikey tips of the giant yucca I'd be wearing armour-plating; but Sacha is made of stern stuff, snipping away with her secateurs wearing nothing but a pair of flip-flops. Yes, our new neighbours are the naturalists. Correction, the nudists.

Postscript

IT'S been six years since I shared that bottle of champagne with Sarah. Since then we've seen and heard from many of our guests. Phil has bought a house nearby. Our American friends write every Christmas, and Allie senior and Douglas are still travelling all over the world. Baby John has two sisters. Joan's husband is increasingly frail, and Michel has moved to England to help her care for him. Barbara conquered her fear of dogs, and she and Martin adopted a rescued Beagle who they named Polly.

As a result of Alison's actions, the people on the corner did make some attempt to improve the conditions in which they keep their animals, but they still glare at us every time we pass.

Soon after her outburst I heard that Ivy's grim little house was burned to the ground. An investigation found that the fairy lights that twinkled day and night had eaten their way through the nylon fluffy cushions around which they were draped. Piles of clothing that lay in heaps on every surface quickly ignited. The plastic pearls, the wigs, the clown, the belly-dancer, the gypsy, the Salvation Army, Annie Oakley, the dressage rider and the flapper costumes all went up in flames in a matter of minutes. Ivy accused her French neighbours of starting the fire, and had to be removed by the gendarmes when she stood in their garden waving a bottle of Beaujolais at them and screaming abuse. She was hospitalised for some time for her own safety, and then disappeared. I thought how much she would have enjoyed relaying the event to anybody who would listen.

I heard that Fliss finally got her man through an Internet dating site, an elderly English widower who bred Bedlington terriers. Soon after they married they moved to Northumberland and that was the last I heard.

What became of Tristram? He moved away, leaving no address. Once, a couple of years later I drove out to the house tucked away in the fields the other side of the woods. It was closed up, deserted, desolate. I'll never know why Beverly left or where he went, whether Tristram ever found him, and what became of them both. An unsolved mystery, an unfinished story. All that is left of them are memories of two beautiful people, some flowers, and an addiction to mint tea.

ACKNOWLEDGEMENTS

TO the friends who encouraged me to record these events, and who helped me when the going got rough, wherever you all may be now, I love you.

Also many thanks to Elle Ford for her inspired artwork.

My appreciation to E-cloths, not only for the way they have helped overcome my fear of cleaning windows and mirrors, but for introducing me to my lovely editor, Stephanie Zia at Blackbird Digital Books. I love working with her. On those frequent occasions when I am utterly lost for the right words, she always pulls them out of the hat. She takes care of all the horrible things like formatting and dealing with uploads, and her patience in coping with some of the frustrations that inevitably occur when dealing with digital media is something that Job would envy.

Respect to Andrew Ives for his meticulous, nay punctilious proofreading. Not an undotted i, not an uncrossed t can escape his eagle eye. He's the man.

And a great big thank you to all those guests who taught me so much about human nature in all its diversity and who left all those pots of jam and pepper behind. We're still enjoying them.

ABOUT THE AUTHOR

Born a Londoner, Susie Kelly spent most of the first 25 years of her life in Kenya. She now lives in south-west France with her husband and assorted animals. She's slightly scatterbrained and believes that compassion, courage and a sense of humour are the three essentials for surviving life in the 21st century. She gets on best with animals, eccentrics, and elderly people.

CONNECT WITH SUSIE KELLY

http://about.me/susie.kelly

MORE SUSIE KELLY BOOKS

Best Foot Forward – A 500-Mile Walk Through Hidden France (Transworld 2000/Blackbird 2011) A touching and inspiring tale of the Texan pioneering spirit, English eccentricity, and two women old enough to know better.

The Valley of Heaven and Hell – Cycling in the Shadow of Marie-Antoinette (Blackbird 2011) Novice cyclist Susie bikes 500 miles through Paris and Versailles, the battlefields of World War 1, the Champagne region and more

Two Steps Backward (Bantam 2004) The trials and tribulations of moving a family and many animals from the UK to a run-down smallholding in SW France.

Travels With Tinkerbelle, 6,000 Miles Around France In A Mechanical Wreck (Blackbird 2012) The author and her husband devised a simple plan – to take a tent and the dog and drive around the perimeter of France. Like many simple plans it went wrong before it started.

The Magic Of France – Memories Of Life And Travel In l'Hexagone (Blackbird 2012) Collected extracts from Susie's writings featuring some of her most memorable times in France.

MORE BLACKBIRD DIGITAL BOOKS

The Dream Theatre by Sarah Ball (2011)

The Born Again Virgin by Stephanie Zia (2011)

The Single Mother's Survival Guide To Sex & Dating by Stephane Zia (2012)

Celebrity Cat Names by Christina Hamilton (2012)

If you've enjoyed this book please would you consider leaving a review on Amazon USA or Amazon UK? A couple of lines is plenty. It really makes all the difference to us small independent publishers who rely on word of mouth to get our books known. Thank you!

Blackbird Digital Books
London
http://blackbird-digitalbooks.com/
blackbird.digibooks@gmail.com

Printed in Great Britain
by Amazon.co.uk, Ltd.,
Marston Gate.